# Lost and Found

## Journey to a Forgotten Railway

David Gridley

Slowcoach Publishing
Canary Wharf
London

First published October 2016

Published by:
Slowcoach Publishing

Printed by:
Lavenham Press Ltd

Distributed by:
Swan Books, 27 Corbets Tey Road,
Upminster, Essex, RM14 2AR

www.swanbooks.co.uk

ISBN: 978-0-9564128-1-2

Artwork by Bill Newman
All photographs are copyright of the author
unless otherwise stated

# Contents

# Acknowledgements

There are many people who have provided me with information and detail for this book and without their input the final product that you are now reading would not be anywhere near as informative and interesting as I hope it has turned out to be. Firstly, I would like to thank both Bill Byford and David Tokeley of Lavenham Press and Jeremy Scott of Swan Books for their invaluable help in explaining all of the intricacies of the book-publishing world; while Bill Newman has once again proved to be an excellent artist and has produced all the sketches within the pages of this book. Special thanks should also go to Simon Atkins whose advice on typesetting and so much more has helped to improve the final appearance of this book.

A big thank you also goes to Marion Siskin, whose patience while proofreading the text has helped to iron out some of the more clunky aspects of this author's approach to written English, and in doing so has greatly improved the final version. I would also like to thank the National Railway Museum in York along with various other research facilities; where hard to come by photographs and maps have been brought to my attention – several of which have made it into the book.

Finally, I would like to thank the people who I met on my journey along this long-lost railway. These people include Madeline Scraggs and her son Stephen, and the many members of the Friends of the Flitch Way who have given me an insight into the work that goes into maintaining the former track-bed. Thanks also go to railway historian Peter Paye and to Ron and Margaret Hutley, who gave me such a warm welcome at their home in Braintree. Finally, I would like to thank Branda and Malcolm Allard for their time and patience during the countless visits that I have made to the railway. Brenda's memories of life on the line during her childhood, her grandfather's long service to the railway and Brenda's own quiet persistence in finally getting Rayne Station recognised as an important historical building, have all helped me to understand why branch lines became such an important part of people's lives. I hope I have done all of you, and the railway, justice in the pages of this book.

Sadly, since this book was written both Ron and Margaret Hutley have died. Ron's contribution to the last chapter was invaluable and although some of our conversations did not make it into the finished book (particularly our discussions of his time serving in World War Two) his love of the railways shone through.

David Gridley
2016

# Maps

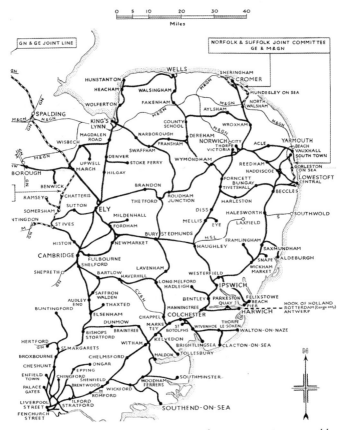

*This map from 1922 shows the East Anglian region criss-crossed by all manner of branch lines (Ian Allan)*

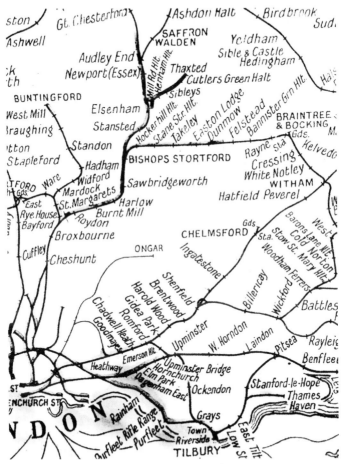

*Map from the early 1900s showing a very busy railway network in the Hertfordshire and Essex regions. Many of these stations have now disappeared (Ian Allan)*

# Timeline of the Bishops Stortford, Dunmow and Braintree Railway

| | |
|---|---|
| 1859 | Railway proposed by local businessmen |
| 1861 | Act of Parliament creates 'Bishops Stortford, Dunmow and Braintree Railway' |
| 1862 | Great Eastern Railway (GER) takes control |
| 1864 | Construction begins |
| 1869 | Line officially opens |
| 1920 | First bus services operate between Bishops Stortford and Great Dunmow |
| 1923 | GER amalgamated into the London and North East Railway (LNER) |
| 1948 | Railway nationalisation sees the end of the LNER and the creation of British Railways |
| 1952 | Removal of passenger service (freight and special services continue) |
| 1957 | Level crossing removed at Easton Lodge Halt |
| 1970 | Braintree to Felsted section of line removed |
| 1972 | Final enthusiasts' trip from Bishops Stortford to Easton Lodge |

# Preface

I think it all began when I was about eight years old. My mother bought me a Hornby train set as a Christmas present and it started a life-long fascination with the railways. It was mounted on a six foot square piece of chipboard and somehow smuggled into our house in the dead of night by Mr and Mrs Copeland, who were long-standing friends of ours. Over the years I bought several sets of engines and coaches, freight wagons, a station and several platforms. I had a couple of steam engines, including a lovely Coronation Scot in vivid scarlet, but on the whole I found myself transfixed by the powerful new diesel locos. In particular I had a soft spot for my Deltic diesel, which pulled a standard set of British Rail coaches; and for the famous InterCity 125, which seemed so sleek and modern back in the mid 1970s.

My little 00 gauge railway world never really got extended beyond the borders of its chipboard base and as far as I can remember I didn't indulge in any shrubbery, trees, shops, bridges or any of the other countless additions that you can make to a model railway. And yet, it was *my* railway – and all the trains ran to time.

I few years later I found myself attempting the art of train-spotting at the end of a windy platform at Euston station in London, although I have to say that I never really took to it. The endless taking down of engine serial numbers until you had captured everything in a particular class of loco (if that is what it is all about) just didn't seem worth all the effort. I am sure it was much more fun in the days of steam engines when the trains were all much more varied and distinctive, but during my childhood steam had long gone and the attraction of waiting for a succession of diesel or electric multiple units (DMUs and EMUs in railway parlance) was simply not strong enough to keep me on a windswept platform. My interest in railways seems to be much more a love of the organisation of such vast schemes. The timetable, routines, maps and even language that is unique to railways has always felt rather welcoming to me.

From the 1840s onwards this novel form of transport created a whole new routine for those people who either worked or travelled on it, and this was to become a way of life with its own particular and very distinctive culture. Perhaps that is why for many years I truly believed that when I got older my ideal job would be to work as a stationmaster at a small branch line station. This station would be in a very rural location, close to a small village with perhaps two or three trains an hour and a smattering of passengers. This idyllic view of the average branch line may have been a long way from the actual reality of life on the railways, but that didn't matter. For a while at least, I believed that a life on the railways would be just perfect for me. In fact, one of my favourite films is the black and white classic, 'Oh, Mr Porter', in which the hapless Will Hay ends up as the stationmaster in the back of beyond village of Buggleskelly in Northern Ireland. Here, along with his bumbling sidekicks Graham Moffatt and Moore Marriott he proceeds to cause chaos along the rural branch line by, among other things, growing prize marrows inside the signal box and drying his wet clothes by stringing a washing line from the semaphore signal! The reality of the early railways was, of course, a far cry from the films of Will Hay and his comic antics; and in particular the pioneering early lines were a dangerous place to be both during their construction and even in the early years of service when accidents were common. Many people died carving out those early railways and many more would end up badly injured before the 'Iron Road' was complete. And yet, it is due to this back-breaking physical effort that the evidence of our railways still exists to this day. Lines that have long ago been closed down can easily be retraced, cutting through the landscape, built up on embankments or crossing valleys with bridges and viaducts. These structures may be crumbling and overgrown but they are still standing, and in doing so they pay tribute to the Victorian pioneers who built them all those years ago.

But a railway is nothing without its trains and my early memories of locomotives all revolve around the power and size of the engines. This is best experienced while standing on the platform and feeling your whole body shake as the engine fires up, ready to pull its heavy load to the destination. I first experienced this in the mid to late 1970s when we used to travel to see my mother's family in Scotland. The overnight sleeper left from Kings Cross station around 10pm and was usually pulled by a Deltic diesel. Originally designed back in the 1950s the Deltics were quite simply the most powerful trains of their time. Running at a top speed of 100mph, its twin Napier engines could generate 3,300 horse power; more than enough to get from London to Edinburgh in under six hours. As a young child I can always remember feeling frightened as we walked past this monster of the railway while we tried to find the sleeping car. Occasionally another Deltic would roar into life; belching a thick black cloud of diesel high into the roof canopy at Kings Cross as the train gently crept out of its platform. A hundred tonnes of engine pulling possibly 10 carriages would take some time to gather speed, but you knew that once it was out on the straight run of the East Coast Mainline its power would finally be unleashed.

Of course, like many people as I got older my interest in

railways fizzled out a bit when first school, then college and finally work left little time for hobbies. My model railway was eventually broken up and thrown away. But my interest in railways remained, and on the odd occasion I would happen to drive close to a disused station or bridge, I just had to get out of the car and take a little look around. Peering over the parapet of a bridge and looking down to see the remains of a branch line that was possibly 150 years old is fascinating to me. It is amazing to think that someone, somewhere had the crazy idea to find the money, pay the navvies, excavate the cuttings, build up the embankments, lay the sleepers and track and ballast, and finally build the stations in such a rural location. All of this to bring those new-fangled steam engines to some of the most remote and quiet corners of the country; places where travel was only really possible either on foot or by horse and cart. All of this was done mainly by hand and without the mechanical excavation techniques that have today made such projects as the Channel Tunnel or Crossrail possible. Maybe these are the reasons that I find railways fascinating.

The audacity and vision of the Victorians to build such a vast railway network would eventually lead to far-reaching changes as this new form of transport set about changing the lives of people who had never really travelled beyond the next village. Suddenly cities like London were within reach and the coast was finally to be explored. The seaside holiday was born when places like Brighton, Margate, Southend and Clacton were all opened up by the railway. Although the movement of people became a great success story for the early railway pioneers, their initial aim was to compete with the canal network for the carriage of heavy goods and in particular the transport of materials that would maintain the Industrial Revolution. In addition, the rural agricultural economy could see major benefits to the new railway networks. If you were a farmer, a miller or a maltster then suddenly all your goods could find a wider range of customers. Heavier loads could be carried further than was ever possible by horse and cart and you could expand your business. And, of course, if you needed to travel to and from work, who knows, you could even become one of the very first commuters. Food distribution was also revolutionised with the coming of the railways. Until the mid 1800s it was impossible for perishable food to be enjoyed by people in towns and cities as there was no means to transport it from its place of origin. Chilling food by means of refrigeration did not become commonplace until the early 1900s, but with the arrival of the railways fresh milk could be transported in milk churns into towns and cities on the early morning milk trains. And the appearance of the humble fish and chip shop on many high streets can be directly attributed to the ability to transport fresh fish quickly around the country from the ports where the fishing boats had landed. Only the railways made these things possible.

Several years ago I compiled a book of walks where the reader could discover many disused railways across Essex. By taking a circular route they could discover various old station buildings, bridges, old level crossings and, of course, the villages and towns that were once served by these now long-lost branch lines. I struggled for a long time to come up with a suitable way to follow it up before the answer became obvious. Instead of writing about many railways I would instead focus on just one. I have chosen the old Bishops Stortford to Braintree line for two reasons. Firstly, this old railway is still for the most part walkable from one end to the other; and this is important as many old lines have now been either built over or returned to private ownership. Often only small sections of an old line will be accessible on foot and this does not make for either a satisfying or complete journey. Secondly, I hope you will read through the pages of this book just what a fascinating railway the Bishops

Stortford to Braintree line was. Built with shaky finances (and for dubious reasons) this old branch has a charm all of its own. Many old railway buildings still exist along the line, as do a few people who either worked or travelled on it. In fact there are still people who work on it. Most of the branch line is now a designated footpath called 'The Flitch Way' and the volunteers who give their time (the Friends of the Flitch Way) have dedicated themselves to both restoring some of the old railway halts along with doing their best to conserve and improve the public footpath while encouraging the natural habitat.

As I embark on my two day journey along the branch as it snakes its way the 18 miles or so through the Essex countryside, there will be a story of royal scandal at the old Easton Lodge Halt, the upset caused by the navvies who built the railway, a secret museum, a ghost station and of course the never-ending battle between railway and road transport, which was to prove to be the slow death of both this and many other branch lines. Although this railway has unique and fascinating stories to tell there is also much about it that in its own small way typifies all that was great about the railway boom, as well as shedding a light on the darker side of this great Victorian innovation that was to eventually bring about its downfall.

This is the story of the rise and fall of the Bishops Stortford to Braintree Railway, but in so many ways it also mirrors the growth and the decline of the railways within the UK as a whole. The twists and turns, and the ups and downs that were a feature along this line were no different to the struggles and achievements that were faced all over the country in branch line Britain. However, this railway, just like all railways, is also the story of railway people. The people who first planned it, those who built it, ran it, travelled on it, work to preserve it, and the many who still enjoy it to this day.

# 1 The 0928 from Bedlam

Day 1, 8am

Back in the 1800s someone coined the phrase 'Cathedrals of Steam' as a way to describe the largest of the early railway termini. Stations such as Paddington, Kings Cross and the vast, Gothic pile at St Pancras would all easily qualify as Cathedrals of Steam, as would York, Liverpool Lime Street and innumerable others. These stations were huge monuments to the coming of the railway age with their high, vaulted roof spaces and had much in common with their religious cousins. In fact, the church bought into the early railways in a big way; putting money into countless schemes across the country and ensuring that most of the big cathedral cities such as Peterborough, Coventry, Salisbury, Ely and Cambridge all became connected to the growing railway network. However, there is one Cathedral of Steam in London that often gets overlooked in favour of its showier rivals. And it is the station where my journey begins. Sitting in the eastern corner of the city of London, within touching distance of the now trendy district of Shoreditch, is Liverpool Street Station. With 18 platforms and over 63 million passengers per year, this is one of London's busiest and most complex stations, serving a great swathe of north and east London plus the greater East Anglian region as well. The station has to somehow incorporate all the surface (or Overground) network with the Circle, District and Central lines of the Underground tube system, plus it is currently excavating a huge below-ground concourse that will house its Crossrail platforms and thereby creating a much needed east-west link right across London.

But at first glance what strikes me as I stand on the corner of Bishopsgate and Liverpool Street is not the railway station itself, which gets increasingly crowded out by multiple skyscrapers, but it is actually the Victorian red brick building on the street corner. This is the Great Eastern Hotel and it is as much a part of railway history as the station itself. Railway hotels and railway termini used to go hand in hand. Every great railway company usually had an even greater, grander railway hotel. Paddington has the Great Western Hotel, Kings Cross has the newly restored Great Northern, Marylebone has the Landmark (formerly Great Central), and of course St Pancras has possibly the most imposing of all London railway hotels in the Gothic masterpiece now called the Renaissance Hotel.

*Like all the other early railway companies the GER built grand hotels to compliment their train services (SSPL)*

All of these impossibly grand buildings were not just built for accommodation. In the early days of railway construction the railway companies needed to show both potential investors and their railway rivals that they were a force to be reckoned with. They had to show that these new railways were going to be a permanent fixture and that they would be a good, safe investment for potential shareholders. The early railways grew so fast that there was very little regulation or law to impede their march forwards and with intense rivalries between competing railway schemes a vast terminal was essential to staking your claim to what many saw as a new promised land. A majestic railway hotel was seen as the obvious accompaniment to a grand station and along with its presence and subconscious statement of strength and permanence it would also perform a very useful service.

*Exterior of the Great Eastern Hotel today*

The Victorians swiftly realised that if people were to be encouraged to take (often quite long) train journeys and possibly stay in towns and cities overnight, then they were going to have to provide safe and comfortable places to stay, eat and possibly sleep. Thus, the railway hotel was born and eventually just about every city, town and seaside location would have one. By encouraging people to use railway hotels it also allowed the railway companies to begin to create a sort of brand awareness with their passengers. They wanted people to associate all aspects of their journey - from arriving at the rural station, to the trains themselves and through to the terminus and its hotel – with their particular railway. Although the train journeys themselves were at least in the early years a cold and uncomfortable experience with open-top carriages, no heating and a hard ride with no proper suspension, the comfort at stations and termini became anything but basic. Railway hotels became grand palaces where (if you could afford it) breakfast, lunch and dinner could reach the level of fine dining. This is a far cry from today's railway experience for most people perhaps, but in the days where taking a train was a new and exciting experience, the railways and all the paraphernalia that grew up around it created a whole new culture and way of life in Victorian Britain.

Today, at Liverpool Street Station the Great Eastern Hotel still stands proud. Smaller than its better-known and grander contemporaries the Great Eastern Hotel is a strikingly beautiful building that has been sadly overlooked for too long. Built between 1884 and 1887 by Charles Barry, this hotel occupies the corner of Bishopsgate and Liverpool Street and originally contained 160 bedrooms. In the late 1800s those wealthy enough could afford a room that had fresh saltwater brought everyday from Harwich for bathing. Thankfully when the hotel was tastefully restored in the late 1990s many of the original features were retained, although you may be glad to hear the bathwater doesn't come from Harwich anymore. Buried deep within the building and surrounded by multicoloured marble, a gilded ceiling and heavy mahogany doors is a secret Masonic temple that seems part Egyptian burial chamber and part Indiana Jones. This 'secret' lodge is just one of many hidden gems contained within the pinkish, red brick exterior of one of London's lesser known railway hotels. The hotel now renamed the Andaz, Liverpool Street, still has an ornate marble staircase which sweeps you down towards the former hotel ballroom. Now a restaurant called 1901 the ballroom has been beautifully restored (it was badly damaged in World War Two) with white marble pillars that reach up towards its domed glass roof. If you fancy a elegant cocktail or two while admiring the stained glass then this is the place to come. Should you wish to visit the hotel for a closer inspection then you may find it being opened up on one of the London Open House events where you can see for yourself some of its remarkable original features. Alternatively the former ballroom still makes for a stylish watering hole if you feel the need to gaze back in time to imagine a far grander period of railway travel while sipping your martini.

However, as much as I would like to spend more time looking around this grand old building I still have to make my way down to platform level to catch my train to East Anglia. However, if you want to see a railway hotel (grand or not) then you only need to look around you. All cities and many towns will have one or maybe more railway hotel located close to the main railway station. Some may have sadly closed down but many still remain, usually in the form of a pub or bar and quite often they will try to keep their railway heritage on display in the form of old photographs or posters scattered around the walls.

Exiting the hotel and heading down a long escalator towards the long line of platforms we come to the other wonder of Liverpool Street – the station itself. But the history of this site actually goes back a long way before the railway came to Liverpool Street. From 1247 until 1676 this was the site of Bethlehem Royal Hospital. Specialising in the treatment of mental illness at a time when little was known about the origins and treatment of such conditions, Bethlem (as it became known) became the unfortunate home to the poor and homeless with all sorts of mental health issues. Some of these had genuine mental illnesses while others could have been suffering from epilepsy or dementia. But with no money and few friends who could help them, they were all were locked away in what became Britain's first mental institution. Patients were often chained or manacled in their cells and the hospital became known as the place where the sane would come to stare at the insane. Hence the word 'bedlam' came into common use. Thankfully the understanding and treatment of mental illness has come on a long way since the early days of Bedlam. The Bethlem Royal Hospital still exists and now occupies another site in London, south of the river. During the excavations for Crossrail at Liverpool Street the Bedlam burial ground was identified. Here archeologists found the remains of over 3,500 skeletons, some of which came from the old hospital but many others did not. Forty seven victims of the Great Plague (1665-66) were buried here. The Crossrail excavations also unearthed the remains of an old Roman road and part of a lost underground river called the Walbrook. These and many other artefacts only came to light due to the extensive earthworks that were required for the Crossrail construction. With most of the major works now complete and the entire project due for completion in 2018, this major feat of civil engineering has unearthed over 2,000 years of London history, and at Liverpool Street it has added several new chapters to the story of this corner of the City of London.

Liverpool Street station is a busy, bustling place at most times of the day. But right now, just after 9am, as commuters begin streaming in from the suburbs, it can seem to verge on chaos. Its 18 platforms and upwards of 63 million passenger entry and exits every year could make it a very congested place. Perhaps the only reason that this vast number of people can navigate their way without the whole thing clogging up is the design and layout of the station. As with the hotel, the station concourse seems to get overlooked in favour of the other, grander designs (St Pancras again) and yet something miraculous has been performed here. As with many London stations, Liverpool Street has been renovated from its original Victorian structure; however, unlike some of its contemporaries the rebuilding work here should be regarded as something of a triumph.

Named after the road on which it sits, Liverpool Street station was originally opened in 1874 after the closure of its poorly located predecessor at Bishopsgate. It originally housed 10 platforms covering some 10 acres of land and cost £2 million to build, which led it to be unkindly dubbed by some as an expensive white elephant. Despite this the station was soon working at capacity and a further expansion of the site was completed by 1895. A key feature at the station was its vast glass roof, which differs from those at Paddington and St Pancras. Those stations have 'span' roofs that arch elegantly over the tracks and platforms below. Paddington has a three span roof while St Pancras has a fabulous single-span roof that was the largest of its kind when built. But Liverpool Street has what is known as a pitched roof, held up at intervals by rows and rows of cast-iron columns. It was very Gothic, very Victorian and at the time unique along-side all other London termini. As Gordon Biddle describes it in his book Victorian Stations; 'With most of its roof glazed, when clean it gave the impression of something between an iron cathedral and a vast Victorian greenhouse. Nothing quite like it had ever been attempted before and it remained unique, transcending even Paddington'.

In more recent times a station modification programme took place between 1985 and 1992 and it is this renovation that is the key to its success as a modern station. Rather than demolishing the old Victorian buildings, many of the older features were cleaned up and incorporated into the require-ments of the new expanded station. And best of all the huge expanse of glass roof was retained, along with the wrought-iron columns that held it aloft. These highly detailed and intricate supports complete with coats of arms and thistle motifs, rise up to the roof and then fan out to form very slender supports that can still safely keep the weighty roof in place. Maybe we should add wrought iron to the long list of great things the Victorians gave us; along with the seaside pier, the city parks, the modern sewage system and, of course, the steam engine. Then having attempted a tasteful renovation the architects and builders had one last masterstroke. High above the main concourse they constructed a mezzanine walkway from which visitors can gaze down onto the hordes of commuters below. It is this raised walkway that allows people to get up close to the roof level, and here you can see some of the detailed designs and patterns that originally went into the construction of the station back in 1874. I can't think of any other London station where you can do this. Paddington may have an amazing roof span but much of the detailing tends to get lost simply because at ground level we are too far from the intricate construction. This ingenious touch at Liverpool Street means that by bringing us nearer to the roof we actually can see the beauty of it more clearly.

*The giant roof space at Liverpool Street is unlike either Paddington or St Pancras*

If only all station renovations were as well executed as this. You only have to look at the brutal concrete box that became Euston Station to see how badly these things can be done.

Opened in 1968 (although the original building dated back to 1837) British Rail's idea of modernisation in the Electric Age never really found favour and has been on the receiving end of much criticism over the years. Thankfully Euston is up for redevelopment and maybe the designers will try to recreate some of the lost original beauty from its early station; maybe even the famous Euston Arch could be brought back. Another positive redevelopment has also been achieved at Kings Cross, where the once cold and windy station has been given a facelift, which managed to add a new ultra modern ticket hall while retaining the train shed and the newly restored Great Northern Hotel.

*From many angles the station resembles a Gothic cathedral*

Finally, any visit to this station would not be complete without spending some time in the corner of the building where both the First and Second World Wars are commemorated. High up on the wall, right next to the McDonalds restaurant there is a large marble memorial to station staff killed while serving in the First World War. The station became famous as one of the first places where high casualties were taken during an early bombing raid in 1917. In all 162 people died and countless others were injured when on a single night a German Gotha fixed-wing aircraft dropped multiple bombs in the Liverpool Street area with the station taking several direct hits. We always think of aerial bombardment as being the product of the Second World War, so it is surprising to find that actually it was being practised many years earlier. Maybe not with such devastation and loss of life as in the years to come, but the psychological impact had been made.

*One of over 100 intricate cast-iron roof supports at the station*

Many years later the station would become the focus of another war effort when thousands of children were evacuated to the countryside from here prior to the German bombing of London in the Second World War. Beginning on 1 September 1939 over 3.5 million people, mainly children, were evacuated from cities all over the UK into the relative safety of rural areas, and this was something that could only be done using railway transport. A few yards from the war memorial there is a statue in remembrance of the famous Kindertransport of 1938-39. Kindertransport (meaning 'children's transport' in German) was the evacuation of up to 10,000 vulnerable children from Europe to the UK prior to the outbreak of war. These children were often unaccompanied and travelled first by boat from mainland Europe to Harwich and then by train to Liverpool Street where they were met by volunteer foster parents. After the war many children tried to a contact their parents or relatives back home only to find that they had been killed in the conflict. However, some children stayed in the UK, made a new home for themselves here and lived out their lives in their newly adopted country. The Kindertransport statue stands just outside the Liverpool Street entrance to the station and is a fitting reminder that the railways can be vital at times of war and can often play a key role; whether that is in transporting people (civilian or military) around the country, or in the movement of heavy loads, munitions or building materials. In the end, this makes the railways valuable both as an asset to the country and as targets for our enemies.

Later in this journey I hope to explore some of what remains of the war effort in relation to the railways, but to do that I first have to jump on to the 0928 service to Cambridge. With ticket in hand I push my way through the paddle gates of platform 11 to board the train, which has only recently disgorged several hundred passengers. It is quiet and empty, apart from the ever-present mound of free newspapers that litter the seats on most morning trains these days. I allow myself one glance back at the station and in doing so it occurs to me that very few of us, whether we are commuters or day-trippers or shoppers, really appreciate just what an important building Liverpool Street Station really is. Overlooked in favour of the glitzier, grander termini along the

Euston Road, this station deserves more than just a second look. Along with the beautiful Great Eastern Hotel, its spectacular Victorian architecture and a history that can be traced back over 2,000 years, Liverpool Street Station deserves its place in history.

# 2 The Working Man's Train

As the train pulls out of the station through a tangle of over-head wires this is probably a good time to detail more of my upcoming journey.

Once I have arrived at Bishops Stortford I will need to pick up a couple of country footpaths that will eventually lead me across the M11 motorway. From here the route of the old railway can be picked up at a place called Start Hill and then it will be a long walk passing Hatfield Forest and the restored halt at Stane Street. From here it is on to the villages of Takeley and Little Canfield and finally passing Easton Lodge station to reach Great Dunmow for an overnight stay. Then day two will head cross-country again to visit the former station at Felsted, another restored halt at Bannister Green and on to Rayne Station. Finally I should reach my destination at Braintree by the late afternoon on day two.

Having done my research I have arranged to meet several people along the old railway including Madeline Craggs, who was the last crossing keeper at Easton Lodge station (she still lives in the crossing keeper's cottage) and Brenda Allard, who has been campaigning for many years to get protected status for the former station at Rayne. I plan to meet several members of the Friends of the Flitch Way who have campaigned to have an old railway carriage perma-nently sited at Rayne Station, which would complement the restoration of the station buildings, which were undertaken by Essex County Council many years ago. And finally I have heard about a man who lives in Braintree and apparently has spent many years building a small and beautiful railway museum in the basement of his terraced house. I don't doubt there will be other interesting characters to meet along the 18 or so miles that I will have to walk on my journey from Bishops Stortford to Braintree over the next two days, and probably more than a few surprises as well.

Liverpool Street station serves a vast swathe of the suburbs of north and east London as well as the main lines further afield into East Anglia to Stansted Airport, Romford and Colchester, plus the seaside towns of Southend, Clacton and Harwich. If you add to that the InterCity trains to both Ipswich and Cambridge then it can be no wonder that by serving the counties of Norfolk, Suffolk, Essex and Cambridgeshire, Liverpool Street is currently London's third busiest railway station. Today services from the station are run under a franchise arrangement with the Department for Transport but my journey is going to take me way back to an era of a very different kind of railway company. This is the time of the railway pioneers.

When you ask anyone to name a great railway company of days gone by, the chances are they will come up with one of four. They will usually say either the London and North East Railway (LNER), London, Midland and Scottish (LMS), Southern Railway (SR) or the Great Western Railway (GWR). However, although each one of these was a truly great railway company, they were not the first. And although they all achieved great things (streamlined locomotives, speed records, non-stop services from London to Scotland, elegant dining cars, electrification) they had one great advantage. All the railway lines had already been built. The big four (LNER, LMS, SR and GWR) came into existence in 1923 under the process of railway grouping, and in doing so they amalgamated all the smaller, independent railway companies that came before. Liverpool Street and all its services came under the ownership of the LNER, but even this name harks back to the smaller railways that it swallowed up. One such company was the Great Eastern Railway and it was this company and many others like it who built the original railway network across the country. But it goes back even further than that. The Great Eastern (or GER) existed between 1862 and 1923, and was itself an amalgamation of several, smaller railways. The GER incorporated the following railways: the Eastern Counties (1839), the Eastern Union (1846) and the Northern and Eastern (1840). It was these three companies, along with their successor the Great Eastern, who were the original pioneers of the railway network throughout East Anglia. They built where there was nothing but open fields, often having to design new engines or carriages as they went. They built the first bridges, tunnels, viaducts, embankments and cuttings. And in doing so they opened up East Anglia to travel and trade.

*Looking towards Bishops Stortford Station around 1911 (SSPL)*

The vast area that the GER came to serve encompasses city and countryside, landlocked and coastal areas, farming and commuting. And if running railways over such a diverse area called for new ideas and innovations, then the GER was to prove itself more than up to the challenge. They designed and built their own locomotives at the giant Stratford Works and pioneered the more compact style of passenger rolling stock that would become essential to the transport of millions of commuters from the suburbs into London. Although they had little need to develop fast, express services, they put a lot of effort into running an efficient commuter service out of Liverpool Street. In 1920, the GER had the distinction of running the most intensive steam powered service ever known; with a peak of 24 trains per hour running on some lines. The GER also pioneered what became known as the 'working man's train' where cheap tickets were offered on specific early morning services. In his book 'Underground, Overground: A Passenger History of the Tube', author Andrew Martin goes as far as to call the Great Eastern Railway: 'The working man's railway par excellence'. He goes on to state that the cheap fares of the GER: 'Were responsible for the great bulge of north-east London, and the growth of Walthamstow, Tottenham and the environs'. While the GER didn't have the money to invest in electrification (unlike the Southern Railway) they obviously knew how to build and run intensive, local steam services and this made Liverpool Street a very busy station indeed.

At the other end of its empire, the GER ran both passenger and goods services to ports at Lowestoft, Felixstowe, Yarmouth and King's Lynn, while the port of Harwich in Essex was developed to allow the company to offer steam boat services to destinations including Rotterdam, the Hook of Holland and Antwerp. The Boat Train Service as it was called, became so popular that passenger numbers grew from 9,350 in 1866 to over 130,000, only a year later; and the GER was to eventually build a new station at Parkstone Quay to accommodate this busy service in 1883. Later the railway was key to the development of seaside towns such as Clacton, Southend, and Yarmouth where the idea of a holiday or short break by the sea was to become a reality for many ordinary people. The Great Eastern Railway also had a few lesser-known and quirky aspects to the service it was expected to offer. For example, the presence of Royal Estate of Sandringham in Norfolk and its local railway station at Wolferton meant that it was the GER's responsibility to oversee the movements of the Royal Train when needed.

Today, sitting in a modern electric multiple unit (or EMU in railway parlance) gliding over the now welded rails that have banished the old clickety-clack many of us used to remember from our childhood, it is almost impossible to imagine how difficult it must have been to build a railway from scratch. Or indeed how dangerous these jobs must have been, especially at a time when health and safety at work would have been all but non-existent and even the early railway laws governing such things had yet to catch up with the rush to build the first railways. Building a railway was a backbreaking business involving dangerous excavations that at times proved deadly for the labourers (or navvies as they were know) who undertook the hardest jobs. Although the terrain in East Anglia was for the most part relatively straightforward to build upon, the construction of large bridges and in particular tunnels could easily prove fatal. But without such people who were prepared to take on these vital excavations, the first railways would never have been built.

The tangle of overhead wires are starting to thin out now as several suburban services peel away. A few local stations have retained their original mid 1800s construction (Hackney Downs for example) but in the main the urban sprawl of north-east London has replaced them with more functional, but far less permanent, modern constructions that often seem to have been bolted onto the older parts with little regard for the overall look of the stations. What were once well-proportioned, even elegant buildings now seem to be strangely unbalanced with little more than a bricked-up doorway or an old piece of intricate cast-iron roofing support to give a hint to their proud past. Picking up speed we roar through first Tottenham Hale and then as the suburbs of London begin to thin out, patches of green start to appear as we pass Cheshunt to reach a leafy corner of Hertfordshire. From here we skirt into Essex for a short while, passing quirky Roydon Mill Station. This grade II listed building dates back to 1844 and is of a low rise, brick and timber construction, which has apparently been converted into an Italian restaurant. However, there is no time to stop as we whistle past the station and rush towards Harlow Town to finally head back into Hertfordshire and the final destination of Bishops Stortford.

*The tangle of overhead wires at today's busy Bishops Stortford Station*

Pulling into the platform I see a forlorn sight. Sitting proudly between the tracks on a red brick base that rises up about 20 feet is the old, timber-framed signal box. With its windows now boarded up against vandalism it still dominates the approach to the station. But once semaphore signals had been replaced and the workings of the points had been taken over by a central signalling centre then the days of this, and many others like it, were well and truly numbered. Most signal boxes were demolished many years ago but some have been saved from the scrapheap to be relocated at railway museums or heritage lines. Here they will be repainted, maybe in the colours of their original railway company, have their levers restored and then see out their days under the watchful eyes of very proud volunteers. But for those that have escaped either demolition or relocation (as here at Bishops Stortford) they seem to exist in a sort of twilight world where they can no longer be used in normal service but at the same time nobody really wants to see them demolished either. So here they sit, gently crumbling, a reminder of a time when the railways were a very heavy and mechanical business.

Bishops Stortford Station (opened in 1842) is another example of a station that has an identity crisis. Dotted around its three platforms are several old Victorian buildings that are presumably listed and therefore cannot be demolished, and they sit alongside more modern structures that neither blend in with the old station or try to create a new architectural style of their own. There is a 1980s style enclosed footbridge plus an ultra-modern ticket hall and retail space that from the roadside resembles a motorway service station. While this busy station obviously needed this renovation to cope with more passengers, you cannot help feeling that not only do the various building styles not complement one another, but also there has been no attempt to try to do so. It is quite possible that the way modern railways are financed and run for the relatively short term that inevitably means a unified style is no longer possible. And while the larger termini of London (Kings Cross, St Pancras) can afford their expensive rebuilding, the single architectural style of the smaller, country stations is in danger of disappearing. No wonder the signal box looks so sad.

Exiting the station and heading up the entrance ramp, a sharp right turn takes me along Station Road and its Victorian warehouses and former shops that were so important to this area. Bishops Stortford is an old market town on the border of Hertfordshire and Essex, about 35 miles from London. As long ago as 1801 the local Corn Exchange enabled farmers and businessmen to trade cereal crops such as wheat and barley, and it is this focus on farming and arable crops that initially helped the town to grow. With the arrival of the mainline railway in 1842 Bishops Stortford began to expand futher, reaching a population of 7,000 by 1901. In more recent times the addition of the M11 motorway (completed 1980) and the expansion of Stansted Airport in the early 1990s, had both helped to increase the population to 38,000 by 2010; with the expectation that it will rise further to 45,000 in the near future. However, I am not going to see much of the town as my walk soon exits the main road and I head off down the wide suburban streets and into the leafier outskirts of Bishops Stortford.

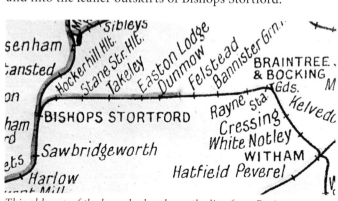

*This old map of the branch also shows the line from Braintree to Witham, which is still open to this day*

Sadly, this first section of the old Bishops Stortford to Braintree Railway has been well and truly demolished. Newly built local roads completely cover the first mile or so of old track-bed until finally the M11 motorway severs any last chance of finding the route of the old branch line. But from that point onwards it will be another story. From the M11 to

Braintree the route will be more or less walkable apart from a small detour around Great Dunmow. But first I have to get to the M11.

*The leafy suburbs of town eventually lead to a footpath across open fields*

The map I have downloaded from the internet clearly indicates that I need to cross a well-tended allotment straight ahead. However, not for the last time on this journey, I get lost. I simply cannot find any trace of a footpath and really don't fancy trampling over somebody's prize onions in the process. Thankfully a couple of gardeners point me in the right direction and after emerging from a small wood I spend the next 30 minutes following footpaths around the edges of several ploughed fields on one of those damp, bright autumn days where, with a bit of luck, a watery sun will break through the clouds and brighten my walk.

At some point here I cross the border from Hertfordshire into Essex and at the brow of the next hill I can hear the roar of the motorway up ahead and discover, thankfully, a small farm track that takes me up and over the M11. The footpath now skirts farming land once again as if to remind me that this part of East Anglia has always been heavily agricultural with a greater dependence on arable crops with the odd cattle farm interspersed here and there. The movement of all this farm produce was to be the initial driver of both this lost railway and many others branch lines across the country. Up ahead I can see a small country lane where I should be able to pick up the old railway and having reached the road I am now looking up at the single arch of an old brick bridge that once carried the railway. This is Start Hill and after climbing the embankment to turn sharp right to head over the bridge, this is the place where my railway walk really begins.

# 3 Skulduggery

Although the Bishops Stortford to Braintree Railway was built in the late 1860s the majority of the railway construction in England took place much earlier. In fact railway building slowly gathered pace from around the late 1820s when George and Robert Stephenson first displayed the locomotive called 'Rocket' at the Rainhill Trials near Liverpool. Then in the mid 1840s there was a sudden surge in railway building that was, within a short space of time, was set to create the vast network of lines that came to dominate the landscape for the next 100 years. This boom in railway construction really took off between 1845 and 1846 and this period has since been dubbed 'Railway Mania' due to the sheer number of new lines that were proposed during this time. Records show that in 1845 alone 2,816 miles of new track were sanctioned, and this was equal to all the lines built between 1821 and 1843. And in 1846 consent was given for an incredible 4,540 miles of track.

This massive boom in railway building also required a equivalent increase in investment as any new railway would be expensive to build; and for this the new railway companies pioneered something called the joint stock company, or what we would today call shareholding. Shares would be offered in a proposed new railway line (often by taking out advertisements in national newspapers) and if successful these new shareholders would be required to pay a deposit to secure their shares. All of this took place even before a sod of earth had been dug on the line.

The directors of new railway companies could be wealthy industrialists, landowners, famous engineers or perhaps even Members of Parliament, and they all extolled the virtues of each proposed new line while giving credibility to the proposed railway simply by their names appearing on the prospectus. The new railway companies were for the most part unregulated and there was little, if any, financial oversight or restriction. In his book 'White-collar crime in modern England' George Robb said 'The phenomenal growth of the Victorian railway network and its accompanying profusion of large corporations gave rise to numerous possibilities for fraud'. And fraud there certainly was.

Proposed railways sometimes collapsed before their passage through Parliament – taking the shareholders' money with it, or once under construction subcontractors might offer payments (or kickbacks) to the directors to secure work, regardless of its quality. Once up and running, a new railway was obliged to hold an annual AGM for supposed inspection of the accounts, but this was wide open to fraud. Auditors were often in the pockets of the directors, a company could be made to look healthy by paying out dividends from the capital, directors could award themselves large payouts when the railway was in fact barely profitable; and all this and more could be done via a system of railway accounting that played into the hands of the dishonest, usually at the expense of the poor shareholder.

A key figure in this period of railway mania was George Hudson. Born in 1800 and a former Yorkshire draper turned banker, Hudson became a prominent railway financier to such an extent that he became known as the 'Railway King'. He was the chairman of several railway companies (including the Eastern Counties Railway and the York and North Midland Railway), was courted by high society and became a Conservative MP. His name only had to be mentioned alongside a proposed railway line for investors to line up, hoping to make huge financial returns. Many of the new shareholders in railway construction were not particularly wealthy and therefore would probably suffer greatly if their investment turned sour. As George Robb recounted, 'Elderly men and women of small fortunes, tradesmen of every order, pensioners and public functionaries, professional men, merchants, country gentlemen – the mania had affected them all'. The trouble was that with no proper financial scrutiny, fraud became rife. Hudson was on the board of several, competing railways with a clear conflict of interest, awarded himself and other directors huge payouts where companies simply didn't have the revenue and perhaps worst of all paid out dividends from the capital of a railway rather than its profits; thereby giving an impression of a company in profit where in fact it was close to bankruptcy. Records show that the Eastern Counties Railway, which was later to champion and give financial support to the Bishops Stortford and Braintree Railway, was continually in a state of financial distress. However, few of the shareholders realised this at the time.

While there were many properly financed projects, a good deal certainly were not and railway mania too often became a bubble of massive financial investment by often poorly informed shareholders into projects that had been proposed by directors often where a good business case for a railway could not possibly be made. Or as The Times newspaper put it, railway mania was 'a tale of national delusion'.

Mismanagement and profiteering became rife on some railways to the extent that often a new line would be proposed solely with the intention of exciting shareholder interest, thereby raising money, only for the project to disappear without trace, along with the initial investment.

As George Robb put it: 'Railway companies were a source of limitless fees for lawyers, engineers and surveyors. It was of little regard to these men whether or not the proposed lines were feasible or the resulting companies successful. Money was to be made simply in drawing up maps, prospectuses and articles of association. An abortive company was almost as valuable to lawyers as a successful one'. Ordinary people began to lose both faith and money as the truth dawned that for the fortunate ones their investment would only bring small rewards in the form of dividends whereas for the less fortunate their investments would disappear completely, taking their hard-earned savings with them. Of course, there were many properly funded railways around the country however, with the Victorian attitude of laissez-faire towards regulating the railway companies, it was probably inevitable that corruption would become rife. Or as The Times put it: 'It was a system without rule, without order, without even a definite morality'.

Eventually, with so many railway companies failing and shareholder anger mounting, the tide began to turn against George Hudson and his fellow directors. In 1849 two major investigations were launched. At the Eastern Counties Railway (which was often found to be on the verge of going bankrupt) Hudson had continued to pay out healthy dividends despite the poor balance sheet. In addition to this a sum of £7,600 had been set aside for what was officially termed 'Parliamentary slush-fund' and at the time this was construed to effectively mean a bribe by another name. The business community was horrified and George Hudson's financial downfall began. Several railway companies now pursued him for fraud and he was effectively exiled abroad to avoid prosecution and jail. Eventually he did return to England, was sent to prison on two different occasions and spent much of his later years fighting various court cases. George Hudson died in 1871.

While George Hudson was an extreme example of the fraud and greed that took hold during the period of railway mania, it is also clear that he was just one of many people who took advantage of that classic combination of events which always seem to be present at times of financial upheaval: a new, poorly understood industry (in this case the railways) poorly advised or informed investors, (shareholders, to you and me) and a lax or non-existent system of regulation. Even after the railway mania bubble had burst, taking with it a lot of enthusiasm for railway investment, Parliament was slow to introduce more effective controls on the financial affairs of companies, and in doing so left the railways to their own devices once again. Another scandal hit the Eastern Counties Railway when it was disclosed in 1855 that the then chairman (David Waddington) had paid out dividends totaling £55,000 when the company revenue only came to £19,000! Reading this, maybe it is not so hard to understand why the ECR was in financial distress for much of its life.

With cases of fraud still occurring regularly on the railways Parliament finally began to clamp down on the worst excesses with the 1868 Regulation of Railways Act, which for the first time laid down a set of standards for the preparation of company accounts. And yet, it is hard to believe that after nearly fifty years of little or no regulation, the railway companies would now become a model of good business practice, even at the Eastern Counties. Later on this journey I hope to meet a man who can shed some light on the reasons why the ECR took up the cause and supported the Bishops Stortford to Braintree Railway. As with many aspects of the early days of the railways, things may not be as straightforward as they seem.

Day 1, 11am

With the roar of the M11 motorway slipping away behind me it is time to make some progress along the old railway. I have about nine miles to cover today before staying overnight in the town of Great Dunmow. This first section of the railway cuts across farmland towards the village of Takeley and for the most part runs parallel to a road called Stane Street. Originally an old Roman road it runs 39 miles from

Braughing in Hertfordshire to Colchester in Essex, and is much quieter now thanks to the A120 bypassing the local villages. As long ago as 1790 Stane Street would have been used by local stagecoaches as they travelled from Great Dunmow to Bishops Stortford, thereby linking up with the main stagecoach route from London to Cambridge. Today, Stane Street is a moderately busy road linking Takeley, Little Canfield and Great Dunmow; but its relatively straight route (being a Roman road) and close proximity to the railway was to prove to be a threat as bus and motor car use became commonplace.

*The route of the trackbed today as it passes Hatfield Forest*

With only the occasional wild rabbit for company the track-bed slowly goes from cutting through open fields into a more overgrown, wooded section as the railway now skirts the edge of ancient Hatfield Forest. It is much darker here as the trees rise on both sides of the footpath and then meet in the middle, high above my head. Several footpaths lead off to my right into the forest itself and if I were not on a tight schedule I would probably venture off to explore this ancient wood. Hatfield Forest is believed to have been turned into a royal hunting forest around 1100 by King Henry I, although mention of it goes back as far as the Doomsday Book. In his book *The Last Forest* (1976) botanist Oliver Rackham described Hatfield as: 'of supreme interest in that all the elements of a medieval forest survive: deer, cattle, coppice woods, pollards, scrub timber trees, grassland and fen. As such it is almost certainly unique in England and possibly the world. Hatfield is the only place where one can step back into the Middle Ages to see, with only a small effort of the imagination, what a forest looked like in use.' In 1924 the forest was given over to the National Trust who continue to manage its 1,000 acres to this day.

*The bleak outlook from Stane Street Halt in 1952*
*(BDJ Walsh)*

The railway cuts across the northern edge of Hatfield Forest for the best part of a mile before emerging on an embankment to reach our first piece of railway history. Here, rebuilt by volunteers, is Stane Street Halt. It consists of little more than a low rectangular, clinker base bordered by railway sleepers, all of which sit at track level. There is a small display board (originally for train timetables) a large name board proclaiming 'Stane Street' – and very little else. Halts were typically built to a bare minimum of both design and cost, with no staff and no buildings, and were usually constructed in an attempt to encourage new passengers to take advantage of a poorly used railway. The Bishops Stortford to Braintree Railway had three such halts built. In 1910 Hockerill Halt was constructed; where the line cut through the Bishops Stortford Golf Club, and was mainly used by golfers, although it was also used by members of the public as well. Then in 1922 a further two halts were built; firstly here at Stane Street and another between the villages of Felsted and Rayne at the little hamlet of Bannister Green.

*The restored halt today*

These last two halts were a valiant, if doomed, attempt to get passengers off of the newly emerging bus services and back onto the railways. If you were a passenger who wanted to alight at Stane Street, then you would need to tell the guard on the train and he would indicate for the driver to stop. And if you were standing on the platform waiting for a train you would need to indicate to the driver (probably by waving) that you wished the train to stop. Otherwise it would go clattering through. Once the train had stopped the guard would lower a set of steps (as the platform was at ground level) and you would be free to either get on or off the service. Tickets were sold on the train by the guard.

Today Hockerill Halt has long since disappeared, however further along the line the volunteer group the Friends of the Flitch Way have set about rebuilding the two remaining halts at Bannister Green and here at Stane Street. Close to Great Dunmow there is the halt at Easton Lodge; however, for reasons that will become apparent later this was built to a much higher standard and for a different purpose. Further on in my journey I hope to meet up with several members of the Friends and hear about their plans for more railway restoration that they have planned for this old branch line. But that will probably be for tomorrow. For today my next stop will be the first station on the line, in the village of Takeley.

*Takeley Station today from the trackside*

Takeley is based around a crossroads of the old Roman road (Stane Street) and a smaller country lane that leads in one direction towards Stansted Airport and in the other heading to Hatfield Broad Oak. Over the years the village has expanded to find itself spread out with small groups of houses springing up along Stane Street either side of the crossroads. Some of these houses back onto the railway, and as they cluster ever closer together a single arch brick bridge crosses the line up ahead to herald the first railway station on the branch.

Takeley Station (opened 1869) is for the most part still intact and the platform, station building and stationmaster's house are in reasonably good condition. The station building itself follows the same architectural styling as the other stations at Great Dunmow, Felsted and Rayne and consists of the main building built in Georgian style which is divided into the booking office, waiting room, lamp room and coal store while the stationmaster's house is also incorporated into the station and is a fine two-storey building with large sash windows and natural stone surrounds.

Takeley and all of the other stations on the branch were built in a style that was to become know as the '1865 type' and was pioneered by the Great Eastern Railway (GER) engineer Robert Sinclair. Sometimes referred to as the 'Essex New Lines,' this surge in railway construction occurred between 1862 and 1868 and saw the development of several new branch lines, all with the same architectural style. Often regarded as handsome and well-proportioned buildings, many examples still exist in East Anglia to this day. In particular the former Central Line (originally GER) stations at Ongar, Blake Hall, North Weald, and Epping are all fine '1865 type' buildings and their modular style, built in either small, medium or large versions are instantly recognisable. Takeley also has the distinction of being one of the few stations to be built from white brick, while all of the others on this branch are of the more traditional red brick that you would associate with many other Victorian buildings. At one time the station also boasted a small goods yard, passing loop and signal box, but sadly they have all long since gone. The Takeley Station building is now used for community events as well as a meeting place for the local parish council.

Now, approximately five miles into the walk, it is time to leave the station behind and follow the old track-bed towards first the hamlet of Little Canfield and then to Easton Lodge Halt and the old crossing keeper's cottage. But my first stop is going to be at the Lion and Lamb pub, which is about half a mile further up the old railway, where I will have a spot of lunch and hope to meet a member of the Great Eastern Railway Society.

*The front of Takeley Station today*

The construction of the Bishops Stortford to Braintree Railway (officially called the Bishops Stortford, Dunmow and Braintree Railway) was to become a difficult and sorry saga. However, the original idea had been a good one. In 1859 local businessmen were looking for a way to transport heavy loads from outlying rural areas into Bishops Stortford where it could be processed further. In particular local millers, coal merchants, farmers and maltsters saw great advantage in finding an easier way to transport their goods than the current slow and inefficient horse and cart. In this particular region of East Anglia the process of malting (turning barley into malt for use in foods such as beer and whisky) was very popular and towns like Dunmow and Braintree all had their own maltings employing many people. In fact Essex probably had a greater concentration of maltings than any other county with over 50 institutions listed.

*Takeley Station in the 1950s (JL Smith)*

After much consideration from Parliament and a good deal of support from the Eastern Counties Railway (ECR) the Bishops Stortford, Dunmow and Braintree Railway finally came into being in July 1861. It would appear that although officially termed an 'independent' railway the reality was that the Bishops Stortford to Braintree was at least partly owned by the ECR and discussions continued between the two with the aim of the ECR eventually taking over this newly established (but so far unconstructed) railway. To add the complication at this time the ECR itself was in its final months of existence as negotiations started to amalgamate several independent East Anglian railways (including the

ECR) into one, large company. The final act was the creation of the Great Eastern Railway in August 1862 whereby the ECR ceased to exist and the vast majority of East Anglia now came under the control of one single railway company for the first time.

Although it was nominally independent the Bishop Stortford to Braintree Railway was in effect in close collaboration with, and financially dependent on, the Great Eastern Railway (GER) for its future. This reliance is quite clear from reading the excellent history of the railway in Peter Paye's book 'The Bishops Stortford, Dunmow and Braintree Branch' where he reports that, 'on the 29th of October 1863, the BSDBR directors were notified of the GER board's decision to subscribe an immediate £40,000 to the company to enable the construction work to commence'. Surveys were now completed, land was purchased for the construction of the line and its stations, and a contractor for the building work was appointed. Finally, on 24 February 1864 a grand ceremony took place at the half way point along the line at Dunmow, where a silver spade was used the 'cut the first sod' of earth and mark the start of the railway construction. By all accounts this was a very grand affair indeed with a public holiday granted in Dunmow and a huge procession of the great and the good through the town and down New Street to the halfway point of the railway. The Chelmsford Chronicle dated 26th February 1864 devoted much of its front page to the event and listed the order of the procession as follows: 'Several navvies bearing flags, the Dunmow Union cadet band, silver spade and mahogany wheelbarrow, 20 navvies, Stortford Union cadet brass band, Dunmow British school, Dunmow national schools, Dunmow private schools, the Vicar of Dunmow and the Directors of the Great Eastern Railway'. The procession was huge with well over 700 people attending; after which there was a banquet for invited guests followed by a ball at the Saracen's Head

Hotel. As the Chelmsford Chronicle put it: 'thus concluded such a series of festivities, and attended by such an influx of respectable company, as has seldom, if ever, been remembered in Dunmow'.

The pomp and ceremony of 'turning the first sod' should have heralded a great future for the new railway; however, the construction phase of the new line was to become (quite literally) bogged down with problems arising over bad weather, contractor payments and land purchases. In particular there were a series of disputes between the Bishops Stortford to Braintree Railway Company and its main contractor, Thomas Brassey. Perpetually short of money, and often requiring injections of cash from the GER, the railway delayed or queried many payments to Brassey, who at this time was employing over 300 navvies to construct the line. It was also quite clear that at various points along the railway formation extra land would have to be purchased as the original survey was far too narrow (at some stations) for construction work to be completed. All of this, plus wet weather, conspired to push back again and again the completion of the line. Clearly this created many problems for the Great Eastern Railway; and a company which was never really on a good financial footing found itself paying out again and again for a branch line that was way over its original budget, and with little hope of getting income from paying passengers in the near future. The Norfolk News of March 1865 reports a GER shareholder meeting where discussing the current railway lines under construction they state: 'The directors have from time to time been most urgent in impressing on those gentlemen (of Brassey and Co) the importance of finishing the lines within the period contracted for'. Even in the dry language of shareholder reports their frustration is clear.

As has been noted during the railway mania period of

railway construction, the awarding of contracts and the individual financial arrangements between company directors and contractors was, to put it mildly, opaque. However, to blame the contractor could well be wide of the mark on this occasion. Thomas Brassey had a formidable reputation in the railway world and unlike George Hudson, it was for all the right reasons.

*Thomas Brassey*

Thomas Brassey (1807-1870) was a great Victorian civil engineering contractor. He won contracts to build many of the railways in Britain as well as constructing lines all over the world including in France, Canada and Australia. His first project was to build the Penkridge Viaduct in Staffordshire and then went on to construct many British railways. Of particular note were the Lancaster and Carlisle Railway, which included the building of the Lune Valley viaduct and the notoriously steep gradient at Shap Fell, and his innovative answer of laying wood and peat rafts to cross the boggy fens of East Anglia for the Great Northern Railway. It is estimated that by 1847 his company was responsible for constructing around one third of all the railways in Britain. Brassey and his company (Brassey and Co) would have been well known to both the Eastern Counties and the Great Eastern Railways as he had worked on the construction of many of their lines including the Epping to Ongar and the Colchester and Ipswich. He also had a reputation for being hardworking with an expectation of work of the highest standards from his employees. A 1969 biography of Brassey states that, 'He was a good judge of men, which enabled him to select the best people to be his agents. He was scrupulously fair with his sub-contractors and kind to his navvies, supporting them financially at their time of need'. At the peak of his career Brassey employed over 80,000 people on four continents.

If Brassey was a great contractor perhaps he was an even greater subcontractor, given that he had a particular way of delegating his work through a network of consulting engineers, engineers, agents, foremen and navvies; all of which allowed him to undertake the vast number of projects he eventually completed. With such a large number of railway projects to deal with it is doubtful

*George Hudson*

if Brassey took any direct control over the building of the Bishops Stortford to Braintree Railway, however his working methods and attention to the quality of workmanship would certainly have been evident on this railway.

Perhaps the greatest insight into the character of Thomas Brassey is the report that on his deathbed at St Leonards-on-Sea in East Sussex in 1870 he was visited by not only his agents and subcontractors but also by many of the navvies who had worked under him. By all accounts some of them had walked for days to pay their respects.

The spiralling cost of the Bishops Stortford to Braintree Railway would seem to boil down to an unrealistic expectation of the true cost of the line from its original inception.

The fact that extra land needed to be purchased at several stations, the goods yards extended at Stortford and a new station built at Braintree were all going to add time, and money, to the project and should have been foreseen at the GER. Their growing financial problems created an atmosphere where contractors' bills were met with suspicion and delay. Between 1865 and 1867 there was claim and counter-claim between the GER and its contractors and yet, slowly but surely, construction continued. By January of 1869 the line had been completed for nearly three years and yet had not officially opened! As Peter Paye reported in his book: 'The rails were rusty, weeds were growing between the sleepers, banks had slipped and the whole system bore and air of decay whilst the parties wrangle over the balance of £15,000 or so'. In the same month the GER finally came to a financial agreement with Brassey whereby he received, amongst other things, £109,000 of shares in the GER as a final payment to cover all outstanding monies.

*A 1958 seaside special service (heading to Clacton) stops at Takeley (Stuart Axe)*

The only problem that remained was that of obtaining the correct safety inspection before the railway could open. Even this took several attempts as the GER had to implement changes demanded by the Board of Trade inspector, who travelled the line on several occasions, including the realignment of track at Takeley Station. But finally, on 20 February 1869, the Bishops Stortford to Braintree Railway received clearance from the Board of Trade inspector to open. From its inception back in 1859 it had taken 10 long years for the Bishops Stortford and Braintree Railway to finally become a reality. Trains could finally run along its 18 miles of single track. And yet, there is still one, nagging question. Given all the financial problems that beset first the Eastern Counties and then its successor the Great Eastern Railway, why would they stick with it? Would it not have been easier just to walk away from the project, rather than to go through ten years of costly overruns? Maybe those old railway companies stuck with the Bishop Stortford to Braintree for another reason.

# 4 Railway Life

'Navvy' is actually shorthand for navigator and was originally used to identify a particular group of hard-working and hard-drinking men who built the navigation canal network from around 1770 to 1830. When the railways came along many navvies made the obvious move from canal to rail construction; swapping one dangerous, back-breaking job for another. And yet, navvies were not just manual labourers. They were highly skilled builders who often worked in dangerous conditions where earthmoving and tunnelling and bridgebuilding was completed for the most part by hand. A typical navvy would be a tough, hard-working character who lived along or very close to the railway that he was building. He would undertake difficult jobs such as excavation and blasting, would probably spend most of his pay in local pubs and taverns, get involved in all sorts of fights and scrapes, and would probably not live beyond his forties. Navvies were highly prized by their contractors (like Thomas Brassey) and they should not be confused with ordinary labourers, many of whom would only work on the railway when there was no farm work to attend to. Navvies lived, worked, drank and slept on the lines they constructed. Once a railway had been completed then navvies would move on to the next site and the whole process of building embankments, cuttings, tunnels, bridges and viaducts would start over again.

Luckily, on the Bishops Stortford to Braintree Railway the terrain was for the most part relatively flat with no need for tunnelling or deep excavations. However, there was one death on the line when in May 1866 a man was crushed under the wheels of several wagons. As the Essex Chronicle reported (in gory detail), 'A young man, named George Bright, attempted, as the men often do, to jump from one truck to another while they were in motion; he missed his foot-hold and fell under the wheels, where five heavy trucks went over him, crushing his arms and breaking three of his ribs, which penetrated his lungs in two or three places. There are faint hopes of his recovery'. Although this was a sad incident, the Bishops Stortford to Braintree got off relatively lightly compared to some. At the Sheffield and Manchester Railway a three-mile tunnel was constructed through the Pennines and during the six years it took to build, 32 navvies were killed and 140 were seriously injured.

Many navvies were originally from Scotland and Ireland and when they arrived in large numbers in rural areas it often caused commotion to the local community. It was not unheard of for navvies to receive their wages in local pubs and sometimes they were at least part-paid in beer. This only encouraged the excess drinking that would all too often lead to brawling or other petty criminality that would end up in court and the local newspaper.

The Chelmsford Chronicle reported in May 1866 that, 'Henry Mills and John Debenham, two navvies lately employed on the new railway works in progress, were examined at the local police station charged with having stolen one lamb of the value of 40 shillings. They were committed for trial'. And here again in June of the same year: 'William Wood, George Wood and William Nutt, all navvies, working on the new railway, summoned for drunkenness and violent behaviour on the 19th May, at Great Dunmow, were each fined £1, 10 shillings, or in default to be committed for one month - Paid'. Finally, in September 1866 (again in the Chronicle) 'Alfred Wood (navvy) was charged by Supt. Rogerson with being drunk and riotous in the High Street on the 22nd of September, and was committed without the option of a fine for seven days'. It would appear that 1866 was a busy year at Dunmow Police Station!

Day 1, 1pm

Less than half a mile up the old railway, about midway between the villages of Takeley and Little Canfield, a foot-path sign directs me a few hundred yards back to Stane Street and the Lion and Lamb pub. Back in 1866 did the navvies frequent this pub? It is quite possible. The railway formation is only a few minutes' walk away and there has been a drinking establishment on this site since 1848 when John Stokes was listed as the 'Beerhouse Keeper'. A beer-house can be seen as the forerunner of today's pub although, as the name suggests, they only sold beer. For payment of two guineas (to the local magistrate) a 'beerhouse keeper' could obtain a licence to sell beer, and often this would be brewed on-site. It is thought that the Beerhouse Act of 1830 was an attempt to deal with the problem of drunkenness in society caused by drinking stronger wine and spirits in the often unregulated 'gin palaces'. Today the Lion and Lamb is no beerhouse. It sits back, off the road, and like many pubs it seems to do a roaring trade in food. Sitting at a small, round table in a corner of the bar is the man I have come here to meet.

Peter Paye is the author of many railway books and is also a member of the Great Eastern Railway Society, which dedicates itself to collecting and keeping alive the history of the GER and its associated railway companies. Through an extensive archive of old documents, many of which are kept at the Essex Record Library, much of the legacy of this old railway company can be traced. Peter started out working for British Rail in 1956 in the booking office at Stratford and eventually worked at Liverpool Street and finally at Waterloo before retiring in 1998 after 42 years of service. He realised he had a fascination for old branch lines and set about writing books on the subject, with his first publica-tion detailing steam engines on the Isle of Wight. Today, he has written 25 rail books with several more awaiting publication. I can only imagine that Peter Paye's house must be crammed from floor to ceiling with all sorts of railway books, notes and photographs. His book, 'The Bishops Stortford, Dunmow and Braintree Branch' is almost an encyclopedic history of this railway, full of detail and historic photographs. However, right now I have a few questions for him regarding the old railway and gazing around the bar my attention is taken by the large number of photographs on the walls, many of which show the local area in a bygone age. In particular there are various pictures relating to the old American Air Force base of Easton Lodge, which was sited less than a mile from where we are sitting.

Peter said "Bombs and munitions were taken by train to Easton Lodge where there were military sidings built in 1942". I am guessing that with military airfields at both Easton Lodge and at Stansted, the area must have come under attack at some point during the war.

Peter continued "The Germans were aware of these movements and on a number of occasions the Luftwaffe attacked the munitions trains on their journeys, in fact a freight train was machine gunned by a German aircraft near Easton Lodge in 1942". Air bases and the railways that supplied them were under constant threat from aerial attack during the war and on one occasion several people died at the Bishops Stortford end of the branch after bombs were dropped from enemy aircraft.

There are a number of memorials to the former American Air Force base in the Easton Lodge area and once I reach Great Dunmow I intend to visit Little Easton Church where I hope to learn a lot more about this small but important airfield. But for now I have another question for Peter. I am curious as to why the Great Eastern Railway supported this rural branch line when they were in such a difficult financial position.

"The GER wanted to block other railways going into East Anglia" Peter said. "So, they grabbed hold of this scheme and built it. But there was no will to push it ahead".

All of a sudden this seems to make sense, and judging by the general lack of morals at the early railway companies it is no great surprise. If you were to look at a map of Essex from around 1865 you would see that about half way up the county, on the right-hand side, the port of Maldon sits close to the Blackwater Estuary and its railway line heads north-east-wards to Witham where it meets the mainline rail services from London to Colchester. From here another branch line heads north-east again to reach Braintree. All of these lines were part of the Great Eastern (GER) network. If a new railway was to head further east from Braintree, through Dunmow to finally reach Bishops Stortford in Hertfordshire then the GER would have effectively cut Essex in half from east to west, thereby stopping any competitor railway from running a service from London into East Anglia.

Peter continued, "It was a political manoeuvre, all the railway companies did it. The Great Eastern Railway wanted to block other schemes going into East Anglia, notably a line going up from Ongar to Bury St Edmunds via Dunmow". "So, this wasn't to do with expanding their railway network?", I asked "No, it was a blocking movement" Peter replied. This would certainly help to explain why the construction of the line took so long, and with poor finances at the GER it was clearly never going to be one of their top priorities.

After a spot of lunch I say farewell to Peter Paye At this point I am about six miles into the journey with another three miles to bring me to Great Dunmow, where I will stay overnight. I leave the Lion and Lamb behind me and take the short hop across Stane Street to bring me back down to the old railway and head towards Little Canfield and then Easton Lodge.

The nature of this walk now begins to change as Stane Street gradually peels away to the left of the railway, taking with it the occasional hum of the traffic, while the smattering of houses that used to back onto the line are few and far between now. This old branch line is taking on a much more rural feel. Disused railways are a haven for wildlife with embankments and hedgerows providing shelter to any number of wild birds and insects. Blackbirds, robins and woodpigeons seem like constant companions throughout much of this stretch of the railway as they feed on the abundance of autumn seeds and fruit that hang from the hedges. Rosehips and hawthorns usually hang heavy with red fruit at this time of year along with the elderflowers and blackberry bushes; all of which give the wild birds some much needed nutrition as winter approaches.

*Overgrown bridge at Little Canfield*

*All Saints Church*

The autumn and winter months are a good time to venture out along a disused railway as the trees and bushes all start to lose their foliage and thereby give a clearer view of the old track formation. The cuttings and embankments begin to give up their secrets at this time of year. In particular this lack of foliage uncovers much of the original navvy-built brickwork, including many of the remaining bridges. It is a testament to the quality of the construction of this railway that even today, some 145 years since it was built, most of its solid structures are still in remarkably good condition. I am reminded of this as I walk over one of the 38 or so bridges that were originally built for the line. This particular bridge crosses a road leading to All Saints Church in Little Canfield and has brick abutments and an iron girder trough into which the track would have been laid. Although it was rebuilt in 1894 this bridge still looks remarkably good for its age; the brickwork shows little sign of erosion and the cast iron, although dark brown with years of rust, could probably still take the weight of a steam engine passing over it.

Most of the bridges on the line were of the brick arch style, including the viaduct at Dunmow, but there were also several (like this one) built with iron-girder troughs. Sadly, the viaduct at Dunmow was demolished many years ago; however, most of the others are still standing proud. With regard to the station buildings, only Dunmow has been completely demolished, while all the others at Takeley, Felsted, Rayne and Braintree are in good condition and can be rightly seen as the legacy of the quality of Victorian construction. This is the same railway construction that took so long to complete back in the late 1860s and had then lain idle for several years while the arguments over money were finally settled. And yet, despite all of the skullduggery, the Bishops Stortford to Braintree Railway did indeed open. Another branch line was born and a little bit of rural East Anglia would see the changes that only a railway could bring.

Usually when a new railway opens you could expect there to be much local interest with crowded platforms and packed trains, or maybe the local dignitaries from Braintree or Dunmow would put in an appearance; but that wasn't to be on this branch line. A combination of bad weather, a general lack of interest from the GER and probable apathy from local people who had seen so many deadlines come and go for the railway, all conspired to keep the numbers attending quite low. From the Act of Parliament that created it in 1862, then the cutting of the first sod in 1864, the end of construction in 1866 and finally the tortuous process that led to the line passing its safety inspection in January 1869, many people had grown weary of the saga of the Bishops Stortford to Braintree Railway.

The first day of service was Monday the 22nd of February 1869. There was a short article in the Essex Standard on the 26 Feb reporting: 'The first train for passengers left Braintree at 07.35 where several availed themselves of a more speedy transit, via Stortford to London. Doubtless there would have been many more, but the only notice given was by a few train lists distributed at the inns, added to which the weather was terribly rough, with snow and rain. The present arrangement is for two trains up and two trains down per day, and three each way on Thursday's.'

The early services ran as 'mixed' trains, which combined several passenger coaches plus assorted goods wagons with finally a brake van at the rear. The addition of goods wagons from the first day of service was an indication to the truly rural nature of this branch line and over time the movement of freight, foodstuffs and livestock would help to supplement the patchy passenger service. However, at least the service was finally up and running. People who had rarely ventured further than the next village finally had the opportunity to travel somewhere new and businesses such as malting would be able to transport more of their goods over much greater distances. People could travel and business could grow.

# 5 By Royal Appointment

'The Prince of Wales paid a hastily arranged private visit to Lord and Lady Brooke, at Easton Lodge. The visit had been kept quiet in the neighbourhood, so as to avoid anything like a demonstration.'

Chelmsford Chronicle, 14 September 1889

Day 1, 3pm

The sun has now broken through the clouds on what is turning out to be a bright, autumn afternoon as the footpath detours around to the left of an old railway bridge whose arch has been filled in with soil to avoid its collapse. Another sharp right turn brings me back onto the track-bed where the slight downhill leads to another minor detour; this time the footpath skirts left to avoid a well-kept garden and I find myself beside a narrow country lane and perhaps the most unusual station of the whole branch line. This is the site of Easton Lodge Halt, and standing proudly beside it is the crossing keeper's cottage. It turns out that the garden I have just detoured around is actually the railway platform and although the waiting room has long since been dismantled, the raised embankment where it once stood is still there. Opposite the old platform, painted in the green and cream colours of the London and North East Railway, is the original wooden hut, which housed the levers that operated the crossing, and beside that is the crossing keeper's cottage itself.

*The crossing keeper's cottage at Easton Lodge as it looks today. The building has changed little over the years*

The hut, garden and cottage all stand right beside the country lane and it is at this spot where the level crossing would have swung open to allow the trains to pass from Takeley behind me to Dunmow up ahead. Although the waiting room and crossing gates are no longer present, the buildings that still remain are key to the story of the Bishops Stortford to Braintree Railway. The fact is that Easton Lodge Halt was not built for any commercial reason, but was only constructed because of the persistence of one woman and her relationship with the future King of England.

Frances Evelyn Maynard was born in 1861 and inherited huge wealth and the family stately home of Easton Lodge, near Dunmow, in 1865. Frances, or 'Daisy' as she was to become affectionately known, was to grow up to become a flamboyant and eccentric figure in high society where her partying was legendary. In 1881 Daisy married Francis Greville in a ceremony at Westminster Abbey where Queen Victoria's son (Prince Leopold) was their best man, and from then on she was known as Daisy Greville, Countess of Warwick. Daisy had many affairs throughout her life and the most famous of these was with Edward, Prince of Wales, who would later become King Edward VII.

This affair (starting around 1886) was to continue on and off for the best part of the next ten years and would have far-reaching consequences for many years to come. It was during her affair with the Prince of Wales that Daisy decided to ask the Great Eastern Railway (GER) to build a station close to her mansion at Easton Lodge and after long negotiations the GER finally agreed to build a halt near Little Canfield. The final cost of building the new halt at Easton Lodge was £140 and as part of the agreement The Earl and Countess of Warwick agreed to pay the sum of £52 per year towards the upkeep of the buildings for the next 10 years.

In August 1895 Easton Lodge Halt officially opened and the Earl and Countess of Warwick alighted a special service from Tottenham, north London. The Essex Chronicle from 6 September stated: 'The new station will open to the public on Monday morning. At present there is one platform, and a small waiting room and ticket office combined, with a man in charge. Trains will only stop when required to take up or set down passengers.'

The single building that housed the waiting room and ticket office was a rectangular wooden construction with large window panes and a sloping roof. By the standards of any of the other halts along this railway Easton Lodge, with its solid structure and the luxury of a 'man in charge', was certainly a cut above the rest.

*'Daisy' Greville, Countess of Warwick in 1899*

But then again, if you have a royal visitor who needs discretion, it is perfect. Some of these visits warranted mention in the local newspapers and the Chronicle from 18 October 1895 noted that: 'On Friday H.R.H. the Prince of Wales paid his usual autumnal weekend visit to the Earl and Countess of Warwick at Easton Lodge. The Prince had been in Newmarket all week and he journeyed by special train to Easton Lodge Station, arriving there at 5.28pm. The Countess of Warwick was in waiting to drive her royal guest to the lodge in a buggy. The little station was for some minutes the scene of bustle and excitement, but there were no demonstrations.'

It is believed that the affair between Daisy and the Prince of Wales ended in 1898, some three years after Easton Lodge Station had opened. And in those intervening three years many royal visits were made to this tiny, rural halt, giving it a notoriety and history that few others can lay claim to. The Prince of Wales became King Edward VII in 1901.

*Easton Lodge and its gardens in the 1900s. Today, only the gardens ramain (Fred Spalding)*

As for Daisy, Countess of Warwick, she later took on the Socialist cause and grew increasingly concerned with poverty in the local area. She sponsored many trade union events at Easton Lodge and moved in left wing literary circles, even renting a house on the estate to the novelist HG Wells. During the First World War she worked for the Red Cross and even welcomed the Russian Revolution in 1917. However, despite her philanthropy Daisy was not good with her own money. After originally agreeing to pay £52 per year towards the upkeep of Easton Lodge Halt, no money was forthcoming for the years 1899 and 1900, leading to much disagreement with the GER. Money, it would seem, was becoming a problem for Daisy. After many years of throwing lavish parties and giving away large sums to worthy (and some not so worthy) causes, she had frittered away much of her vast inheritance and by 1928 was left nearly bankrupt and under the threat of prison. Ten years later Daisy, Countess of Warwick died, aged 76.

*Easton Lodge Halt platform view. Above, from the early 1900s (Lens of Sutton) and below the same view today*

Level crossings, like the one at Easton Lodge, were very common in the early days of the railways as most roads or country lanes were exceptionally quiet. At a time when the motor car was yet to be invented, it simply didn't make sense to build expensive bridges for the quieter country lanes where (like here at High Cross Lane) the very light traffic only consisted of the occasional horse and cart or maybe a few locals on foot. And so, the manually operated level crossing with its twin gates that would be swung across the road by the crossing keeper to let a train pass, became a familiar sight all across the country.

Many level crossings were in remote and rural locations and combined with the often infrequent branch line services this meant that staffing levels were always quite low. Here at Easton Lodge there were only two members of staff: a porter-in-charge and the crossing keeper. It is unsure who the original porter-in-charge was back in 1895, although records do show that a lady called Hannah Ward was the first gatekeeper. From 1899, Charles William Green was the porter-in-charge until his retirement in 1911. Local newspapers reported that: 'He is about to retire on pension from the service of the Great Eastern Railway. Mr Green has always been regarded with esteem by those with whom his business brought them into contact'.

Photographs taken during his service show a delightfully Victorian looking man, standing tall in his gold-buttoned uniform, with a bushy, white moustache. Like many railway workers Charles Green gave most of his working life to the railway. He retired at the age of 67, having been employed for over 50 years at various stations in East Anglia, and so must have started working on the railways when he was 15 or 16 years old. A long and distinguished service was commonplace for many railway workers and it was quite normal to find families where railway employment would go back several generations, father to son and so on.

Sadly the porter-in-charge job was phased out in the 1920s

when guards began issuing tickets on board the trains, leaving Easton Lodge with only a crossing keeper. However, this job remained important for many years to come as railway sidings were built to accommodate firstly military stores for the American Air Force base at nearby Easton Lodge, and then later a banana processing plant was sited just behind the crossing keeper's cottage and this made use of the railway sidings to transport its cargo.

Today, standing in front of the former Easton Lodge Halt, it is not difficult to imagine all the coming and going of high society at this rural location many years ago. The royal carriage drawing into the platform, the sporadic passenger service with seven trains each way at its peak, the military trains in the Second World War, and then later the goods traffic. Without much effort at all, I can see porter-in-charge Charles Green filling the oil lamps that kept the platform lit as the sun went down.

Yes, some things have changed here at Easton Lodge but much remains the same as well and although the platform and waiting room have gone and the crossing gates long since been removed, the cottage and its garden have changed remarkably little since the Victorian era. The crossing keeper's cottage is a very familiar building and shares a lot of the same architecture at Takeley Station, a few miles away. It was built in the same '1865' style as all of the stations on the branch except that, being a cottage and not a station, it is a small two-up and two-down building. It was built from the same white brick that was used at Takeley and has the familiar Georgian style of large, sash windows with heavy stone surrounds that identify all of the stations on this railway. The lady who now lives in the cottage has also seen many years of railway service. In fact, Madeline Scraggs was the very last crossing keeper here at Easton Lodge, and I hope she will be able to tell me something about the life of this railway.

We are sitting in the front room of the cottage and my eye immediately is drawn to the open fireplace and the old range cooker that sits within it. This house does not appear to have changed very much over the years.

"The council came to look at the cottage with a view to installing central heating, but that was two years ago!" Madeline explained. "Although, I don't think I would want it anyway – think of the mess."

Madeline is in her early eighties now, with a good head of bright white hair and a kind face. This cottage has been her home for the last 50 years.

She continued, "I came here to work as the crossing keeper in 1961. At the time my husband Fred had been on the railways for 20 years, working as first a locomotive shunter and then an inspector. By the time I arrived here it was all freight trains as the passenger service had long gone."

Was there much in the way of freight, I asked.

"At that time there were only four trains a day, and these came from the sugar beet factory at Felsted. But there were more trains from 1962 onwards when the banana factory opened here at Easton Lodge."

Today, the factory is still operating but all of its goods are transported in and out by lorry. As we sit here the occasional rumble of a HGV along the lane announces another delivery.

I ask Madeline about the process of gatekeeping. How did she know a train was approaching?

"When a train left either Dunmow on one side of us or Takeley on the other, a message would be telegraphed to a bell outside the cottage, and it would ring to catch my attention. Then I would go out and open the double gates for the train to pass. The bell is still there you know."

We go outside the cottage and sure enough, attached to the side of the lever hut, there is a double bell with its rusty hammer in the middle. Of course, if the ringing bell was missed for some reason then a crash could easily occur. There is a story told that during the late 1890 or early 1900s, a relief gatekeeper overslept one morning with the result that the first goods train of the day smashed through the crossing gates!

Today, almost all manually operated level crossings around the country have been phased out in favour of electronic barriers. Those that do remain are mostly to be found in East Anglia, particularly in Norfolk and Lincolnshire but even these are living on borrowed time. Soon the job of crossing keeper will be relegated to railway history.

I asked Madeline when her days as crossing keeper came to an end.

"It was 1965, and British Rail decided to do away with the job of crossing keeper and leave it to the crew of the freight trains to stop and open the gates by themselves. I was then transferred to Dunmow station until that closed as well."

From that very first day in 1961 right up until the present, Madeline has continued to live here at the old crossing keeper's cottage at Easton Lodge. She tends to her garden, chats to the occasional railway enthusiasts who turn up to look at the old halt and does her best to preserve this little piece of railway history. Perhaps because of the royal connection the cottage is now a listed building and thankfully there are restrictions on any alterations or renovation that can be done here, and maybe that explains the reluctance of the local council to undertake any building work on this old cottage. But whatever the reason, Madeline seems quite happy to leave things just as they are.

"I couldn't live in a posh, up-to-date house," she says, "that's not for me." She seems very contented here, and even without the trappings of modern living, a railway cottage does have a special feel to it. I wonder if she feels the same way?

"Crumbs, yes! I couldn't live anywhere else."

I wave goodbye and leave her standing under the porch of her cottage, as I cross the lane to follow the footpath and the route of the old branch line. Up ahead the A120 dual carriageway now effectively cuts right across the old railway and so to keep the walk continuous, Essex County Council have installed a footbridge which takes me up and over the road. Once on the other side the railway cuts through more arable farmland and will eventually take me the mile or so to reach Great Dunmow at the end of my first day. But right now I am going to see some of the conservation that has been undertaken along the old branch, and the people who make it happen.

Up ahead I can see a work party, which has just finished for the day. The five people, complete with wellington boots, tough trousers and green fleeces are packing away, and in the distance there is a smouldering fire with brambles and grass cuttings piled atop. These are just a few of the volunteers from the conservation group called the Friends of the Flitch Way and every Tuesday and Thursday they venture out somewhere along the railway for a day of restoration work. Ever since Essex County Council designated the old branch line an official country park in 1989, there has been a need to maintain the 15 miles or so of almost uninterrupted railway formation, all the way from Braintree to Start Hill, near Bishops Stortford. After all, just calling an area a country park does not in itself protect or enhance an area. For that you need a plan and people who understand how to develop and enhance the landscape. And so, in 2004 a group of local people who were interested in protecting the old railway and the natural life that lives along it came together to form the Friends of the Flitch Way.

Ever since then, these Friends have worked tirelessly not just to encourage local wildlife by building new habitats for birds, insects and plants but they have also been instrumental in making sure that the old railway and its history are not forgotten. It is the Friends who have created walkways on the old track-bed, installed benches at beauty spots and rebuilt the halts at both Stane Street and Bannister Green. The Friends even have an ambitious project to bring an old railway carriage to Rayne Station, where it will be permanently sited beside the old platform. The plan is for the carriage to house both an extension to the café and a small museum, where the history of the railway can be explored by visitors.

The Friends now work in conjunction with the local park rangers who can provide professional advice on such things as what to plant and where, coppicing of trees and pond maintenance. Further up the line I hope to meet with the current chairman of the Friends, Stan Davies and discuss the various projects they have been working on. But that is several miles away, at Bannister Green Halt and will be part of tomorrow's journey. Right now my walk takes me through one of the most beautiful parts of the railway as I enter an area called Dunmow Cutting.

As its name suggests, the final stretch of the line as it approaches Dunmow had originally been cut into a gently sloping hillside to avoid any steep gradients. This has helped to give the landscape a valley-like appearance where, with careful tending by the Friends, a haven for wildflowers and butterflies has been created where once there was a simple railway cutting. It makes you realise, that with a little help, abandoned railways can be the perfect place for wildlife to flourish. Cuttings and their polar opposite, embankments, offer contrasting and yet ideal conditions for all sorts of wild animals and plants. A high-sided embankment will offer a more enclosed habitat where the narrow railway formation will often be bordered by trees and shrubs, this offers both a home to animals as well as providing protection from predators. An excellent example of this would be common trackside plants like blackberry or hawthorn, whose prickly stems and dense foliage allow many small birds and mammals to find not only safety but food as well. The hawthorn has a dense covering of white flowers in the spring (good for bees and other insects) which will usually be followed in the autumn by a heavy crop of the dark red berries that will be much needed by wild birds in the bleak winter months. The blackberry has exactly the same benefits to wildlife (and to humans if you have ever been blackberry picking) and it will also spread its impenetrable, thorny foliage over a large area, thereby providing a home to countless animals.

On the other hand a railway cutting will give a different, but equally diverse habitat for wildlife. A cutting is not usually as narrow in width as an embankment and the trees and shrubs may be limited to the upper reaches of its slopes. This will leave a wide valley with the railway at its base, allowing the sunlight to attract many different animals and plants. In particular grasses, thistles, buttercups and numerous wildflowers will grow on the sunlit slopes of a cutting and these will in turn attract butterflies, grasshoppers and other insects.

As I walk through Dunmow Cutting in the autumn, the best of the wildflowers have long gone and yet there is still something lovely about this part of the old railway. Maybe it is the peace and quiet that the cutting creates, or perhaps it's that slightly sweet smell of the grass cuttings from today's work party. Either way this secluded cutting finally comes to an abrupt end as I pass through the middle arch of an old three-arch brick bridge to emerge in a wetland area called the Boardwalk. Here small streams bubble up either side of the footpath as a well-laid set of duckboards mark the way ahead and I venture through a land of moss and ferns, dragonflies and beetles. Where the cutting was bright and open, the boardwalk is much more dank and enclosed. The canopy of trees overhead is thicker now, and this along with the running water helps to keep everything at ground level damp in this final stretch of railway before Dunmow.

*Nature has slowly started to reclaim this old bridge on the Flitch Way*

In the last mile or so I have travelled through an incredible variety of wildlife habitats, ranging from embankments to cuttings, arable farmland to wet woodlands. Much of it is unique and owes its diversity to the simple practicalities of railway construction and the basic fact that a railway needs to be built on flat (or relatively flat) ground. And whereas some gentle gradients are acceptable, for the most part engineers will try to iron out any excessive uphill or downhill sections by using either embankments or cuttings to level out a railway. It is these two mainstays of railway building, the cutting and the embankment, which have managed to create two different wildlife environments, both hosting their own little ecosystems. Finally, another by-product of railway construction that enhanced its attraction to wildlife was the planting of trees and shrubs to essentially hold any newly built railway together. Any freshly built embankment or cutting would be prone to landslip unless the soil could be made to stay in place, especially after heavy rain. It is for this reason that railway builders to this day plant a mixture of grasses, shrubs and trees along a railway formation as a way of strengthening its construction. On a railway that still operates, this vegetation will be cut back at regular intervals so it does not interfere with the day-to-day running of trains, but on a disused branch line the wildlife will be left to its own devices. Over time it will continue to grow unchecked, encouraging more birds and insects, and plants.

With careful maintenance of this old railway the Friends of the Flitch Way have managed the tricky balancing act of both allowing the wildlife to thrive as well as keeping the footpath open for all. This is 15 miles of footpath and country park and disused railway - all rolled into one, and somehow this group of determined volunteers manage to maintain all of these elements to make sure that this unique habitat is not lost.

*Dunmow today is a fine example of a traditional East Anglian town*

Day 1, 5.30pm

The old railway now emerges onto a road on the outskirts of Great Dunmow and it is at this point that I will have to detour through the town to pick up the footpath afresh tomorrow morning. This road (called Dunmow Bypass) almost exactly follows the route of the old railway and it therefore forces me to venture into town to eventually reach the spot where Dunmow Railway Station once stood. Sadly, nothing remains of the station building or its signal box and goods yard. The only hint that this town once hosted the largest station on the branch line is the fact that its approach, Station Road, still exists and its name can still be found embossed onto a couple of road signs in the area.

I now take the short walk through the small back alleys of Dunmow to bring me to my bed for the night at the Saracen's Head Hotel, on the high street. But before I make myself comfortable at this old coaching inn I have one final visit to make before I retire for the night.

A short taxi ride out of Dunmow brings me to the tiny village of Little Easton and its parish church, which sits on higher ground along a country lane. This well kept church, parts of which date back to the 13th century, is constructed in the typical stone and flint Norman style. It is thought to be on the site of a previous Saxon church with some evidence of Roman occupation as well (look out for Roman bricks within the current construction). There is a small clutch of old houses to one side of the church and further down the lane is what remains of Easton Lodge House, formerly owned by Daisy, Countess of Warwick, way back in the days of her affair with Prince Edward VII. After a disastrous fire in 1918 only the west wing of the house has been preserved and this, along with its impressive gardens are the sole survivors of a once grand Gothic stately home.

*The American Airforce memorial chapel*

During the Second World War the house and its large estate was requisitioned by the British Army who in turn gave the land over to the American Air Force for the construction of an airfield. As the railway historian Peter Paye has already mentioned (page 48) the Bishops Stortford to Braintree Railway was used to supply the ammunition and armaments to both this airfield and its close neighbour at Stansted but it is also true that much of the building material for both bases came in via the railway too. The railway network across the country became vital to the war effort, whether that was in carrying the building materials to construct military bases, supplying bombs and ammunition, moving large numbers of troops, transporting food and produce, or even the mass evacuation of children from the cities into rural areas. None of these things could have been undertaken without the help of the railways, and this small 18 miles of track in rural East Anglia played an important role in what was often called 'the war effort'.

*Little Easton Church*

From September 1943 the United States Army Air Force (USAAF) based its 386th bomber group at Easton Lodge and it is from here that its B-26 Marauder aircraft would fly on missions to France to bomb enemy airfields, railway marshalling yards and even in some instances, V2 rocket launch sites. The B-26 was a medium-size, twin-engine bomber that was designed to fly up to 3,000 miles without refuelling with a 5000lb bomb load. It had two machine gun positions: one in the nose and another just in front of the tail fin. Although the B-26 had formidable firepower it also had a reputation as a difficult plane to fly. Its engines had to be maintained to exact standards and it had a relatively fast landing speed of 150mph, making a landing at a short runway particularly tricky. For these and other reasons the B-26 gained the unfortunate nickname of the 'widowmaker' despite the fact that they made an invaluable contribution during the war.

Many B-26 Marauder missions were flown from the airfield at Great Dunmow and General Eisenhower visited the base in 1944 during a tour of local airfields. With the end of the war came the closure of many, smaller airfields across the country and the USAAF finally left Easton Lodge in August 1945, with the base finally closing three years later. It is amazing to think that by the end of the war East Anglia contained over 100 RAF/USAAF airfields of which 14 were in Essex. Many of those, like Easton Lodge, were closed and either built over or left for nature to reclaim them. Of the others, several still exist as private airfields (such as North Weald) while the occasional one has expanded and become a modern, international airport – just as Stansted as done.

While Easton Lodge may have closed in 1948 and the land turned over to agricultural use, the ties of friendship made during conflict were clearly very strong between the airmen and the local inhabitants of Little Easton and Great Dunmow. To this day there are reminders of the sacrifices that were made during wartime and also reminders of enduring friendship. There is a brick and stone war memorial on the main road at Little Canfield where the inscription reads "In memory of our gallant brothers and comrades who never returned from the air war over occupied Europe". This is followed by a list of dozens of US airmen who died in combat. And just a few hundred yards from the site of the airfield, Little Easton Church has a dedicated American Memorial Chapel, containing two large stained glass windows depicting friendship and peace. This is contemporary stained glass, showing both airmen and soldiers from the United Kingdom and the USA with various references to the old airfield. Somehow this modern addition to what is an old Norman church does not seem out of place. Perhaps it is the peaceful setting (looking as if it has not changed for many hundreds of years) that encourages visitors to think back to a time, not so long ago, when things were very different.

# 6 Malt and Barley

The small market town of Great Dunmow sits almost exactly midway between Bishops Stortford and Braintree and marks the halfway point of the old railway. There is evidence of settlement in Dunmow as long ago as the Bronze and Iron Ages and both pottery and coins have been found from Roman times (the old Roman road Stane Street ran through here). The first use of the name Dunmow seems to arise around AD950 when the word 'Dunemowe', meaning 'meadow on a hill' started to crop up.

The town sits in the Chelmer Valley with the High Street sitting on higher ground while the area known as Church End grew up along the valley floor by the river, and by 1086 there were 674 families living in the area. In the 12th century the town was granted a 'market charter' whereby regular markets and fairs could be held at a designated time and place. Dunmow was one of many towns across the country to be assigned a market charter (others included Market Drayton, Market Deeping etc) all with the purpose of encouraging trade, especially in the agricultural and farming regions where many people were employed. With this newly acquired market status the development of the town moved away from the river (and the possibility of flooding) to higher ground. To this day Dunmow still has a road called Market Place, and it is here at its wide junction with the High Street that buyers and sellers of goods would have gathered on market day for hundreds of years, overlooked by the 16th century town hall. Local records from 1671 noted that the market traders included; 'searchers and sealers of leather, flesh and fish, ale tasters and bread weighers'.

Together with its bustling market, Dunmow also had a thriving cloth and tanning industry, a maltings and many local shops including drapers and cheesemongers. The town also had a savings bank. In addition there was a corn dealer, timber merchant, tea dealer, boot maker, printer, chimney sweep, beer retailer and a baker. All of which helped the town to grow in both size and population. In 1801 Dunmow had 1,800 residents and the arrival of the railway in 1869 would have only increased this further until 1901 when the number had risen to 2,700.

Today, many of these old businesses have sadly long gone, not just from Dunmow, but also from countless towns across the country. Some (like chimney sweeps) have disappeared simply because they are no longer needed while others have found the march of time and progress have made their small-scale enterprises uneconomic. Tanning leather for example is now for the most part a mass-produced and high volume industry and not a small, back-street operation involving barrels and acrid smelling chemicals. And malting, while still an important industry, has developed from the days of small, independent producers to become a business of scale where the large brewing companies dominate the market.

However, even though many of the more traditional trades have disappeared from this and every other town, there is a legacy left behind. Usually it is the buildings where this can be found. The centre of Dunmow is now a conservation area and the area around the High Street, Market Place and North Street is full of listed and preserved buildings. In fact, the greater Dunmow area contains no fewer than 250 listed building, 170 of which are in the conservation area.

It is in the middle of this conservation area that I find myself, as I stare out of the window from the restaurant of the Saracen's Head Hotel at the start of day two of my journey. The hotel sits on the High Street facing out directly onto the Market Place and is (not surprisingly) a listed building. An old coaching inn, from the days when stagecoaches were the only way people could travel between towns and cities, the

Saracen's Head has been tastefully restored in recent years with plenty of low ceilings and exposed woodwork still on display. Of course, way back in February 1864 this was the venue for a grand evening ball to celebrate the ceremonial 'cutting of the first sod' of the new railway. This event was described in great detail by the Chelmsford Chronicle, where the evening's festivities; 'Took place at 9 o'clock and was a select affair, at which about 100 were present. The room was very beautifully and artistically decorated in special keeping with the occasion. Above the entrance was an elevated orchestra and the supper-room was prettily decorated in laurel and evergreens and the ante-room illuminated with numerous Chinese lanterns. Dancing to the delicious strains of Pratt's excellent quadrille band was kept up till a late or rather to an early hour…'

*The Doctor's Pond in Dunmow*

Sitting here over a hearty breakfast it is hard to imagine just how grand an occasion this would have been or indeed how impressive the sight of this whole affair must have made to the locals of Dunmow. After all, a holiday had been declared on this day and literally hundreds of people had turned out to witness everything from the cutting of the sod, then the procession through the streets, the banquet with all the speeches, the concert at the Town Hall and finally the ball at the Saracen's Head. This was a truly grand event by any standards. This must have raised the expectations among the locals that the coming of the railway was, if not imminent, then at least within reach. Sadly, as we now know, the five years between the 'cutting of the first sod' and the first day of train service (in 1869) was to be somewhat at odds with the initial promise of the railway. Maybe this ability to throw a lavish event in Dunmow and yet wrangle for so long over the actual construction of this branch line tells us more about the misplaced priorities and parlous financial state the Great Eastern Railway than anything else.

After checking out of the hotel I cross Market Place and head towards a very old building, which I hope will show exactly why the Bishops Stortford to Braintree Railway was proposed in the first place. My plan for today will be to head out of town to pick up the route of the railway as it heads cross-country towards Felsted and its old station. Then I will return to the Flitch Way footpath and head for the old halt at Bannister Green where I hope to meet up with some of the Friends of the Flitch Way. From here it will be a long walk towards Rayne station and its café, and then the final stretch of the footpath will lead me into Braintree where I can pick up the train service back into Liverpool Street. Probably nine miles in all; and hopefully most of it will be under this bright blue, cloudless sky, which casts hard shadows from the overhanging buildings around the ginnels in town. Ginnels are small alleyways that usually run between buildings at right angles to the main road. They are more common in northern towns but they can be found almost anywhere. Here in Dunmow there are several such ginnels running off of the High Street and they, along with the sheer number of historic building, help to retain the ancient street pattern of this town. Dunmow can be seen as an excellent example of an ancient East Anglian town where the building styles and construction methods are so typical of their period. In particular the Essex style of timber-framed buildings with steep, tiled roofs are in abundance and it is this along with other techniques such as pargeting and weatherboarding which give this whole area of north Essex and much of East Anglia its distinctive character.

This doesn't necessarily mean there has not been change in Dunmow and over the years there have been several small housing developments dotted around town. Currently there are plans to expand the town much further with a large development of new houses on the outskirts of town, which worries many local people who fear the character of the area will inevitably be lost. However, manageable growth would surely be a good thing if it were to bring new people to visit the shops along the high street. Dunmow still has a long way to go in growth terms to catch up with the other towns in the area that have kept their railway stations. It is striking to see the difference between places such as Halstead, Dunmow or Maldon (all of whom have lost their railways) and others like Braintree, Witham or Chelmsford who have all increased their populations considerably for the simple reason that a railway will attract growth. But expansion in Dunmow today is not driven by the railway. It is instead driven by motorised transport: the car, the lorry, the bus and the coach. And it is the pressure to accommodate the needs of motorised transport that is forcing places like Dunmow to consider expanding beyond anything they have had to consider before. The outcome of this is unpredictable. But let's not forget that this town has been through expansion before, when the railway first arrived here on 22 February 1869. There must have been worries about what the new railway might do to the character of town even then. But whatever worries there were seem to have been forgotten as prosperity grew and business flourished. In particular, the boost that the farming sector received with the opening of the railway cannot be overstated.

The original push for building the Bishops Stortford to Braintree Railway had come from local businesses and in particular those in Stortford who wanted agricultural produce brought in bulk from the outlying rural areas surrounding Dunmow. In East Anglia this could mean many products including sugar beet, corn, wheat and barley. And it is barley that brings me to this rather odd-shaped building, only a few hundred yards from the centre of town. This is Dunmow Maltings; a 16th century timber-framed building, which produced malt up until the 1940s. It is a two-story rectangular structure with a tiled roof and a conical-shaped air vent that pokes up skywards as if it has been forced up, through the tiles. Similar vents can be seen on historic oast houses in Kent and were used to draw hot air up and away from the kiln below. Today, the maltings has been restored and turned into the local museum housing all sorts of artefacts from antique clocks to a full-size horse-drawn fire engine. I am sitting in part of the museum exhibition, surrounded by glass display cabinets while above me the white painted beams of the first floor bow and push down from an already low ceiling.

The process of malting barley is essentially the same today as it has been for hundreds of years. Techniques may have improved and the scale of production may have increased hugely but the basic principle is the same today as it was for the Romans. Barley is gathered from local farms and brought to the maltings where it is soaked in water for several days. After the water is drained away the barley is spread evenly across the floor of the building by the maltster; it will then be regularly turned by shovel for anything up to a week until the seeds start to grow roots and shoots to begin the process of germination. At this point the natural starch in the barley has begun to turn to sugar and it is this sugar along with water and yeast that will form the basis of beer production. Now the whole consignment of barley is moved into the kiln where it is spread across a wide floor consisting of clay tiles, all of which are perforated to allow heat to rise from below. This heating, for anything up to another seven days, brings a halt to the germination process and thereby locks in the sugar content of the barley. The roots and shoot are now knocked off the grains (and may be sent back to farms as animal feed) and the remaining malt is now poured into sacks, ready for transport to brewers in the region. In the case of the Dunmow Maltings, most of their malted barley was destined to go to Bishops Stortford where many brewers had premises for the production of ale and porter.

Although this process of turning barley into malt sounds fairly straightforward, there was actually a great deal of skill required and in particular the regulation of the temperature and time that the barley spent in the kiln would create flavour variations which could be exploited later. The distinctive beers that became popular in the 18th and 19th centuries (known as porter and stout) all derived in part from the degree of roasting that they received in the kilns of a malthouse by the skilled maltster.

Today the terms beer, lager, ale, porter and stout have become somewhat intertwined, but in general terms a lighter beer (like lager) would come from a lightly roasted malt whereas the longer-roasted, and darker malts would give you a porter, while a stout, like Guinness, is darker still and usually has a higher alcohol content. It is not only beer that relies on malt as one of its basic ingredients. Whisky (think of single or double malt) also requires malt from barley, as does malt vinegar, malt loaf and malted milkshakes. Rich tea biscuits and brands such as Horlicks, Ovaltine and Maltesers all rely on the malting process. And let's not forget the vile syrup called 'cod liver oil and malt' which some of us were force-fed in our childhood, supposedly as a way of improving the taste of cod liver oil – which it didn't!

*Dunmow Maltings is now a museum*

Dunmow Maltings was just one of dozens of malt houses that grew up across East Anglia to cater for the ever-growing need of malt-based products, and the arrival of the railway network meant that larger loads could be carried over greater distances. It wasn't just barley that benefited from the railways; other cereal crops such as wheat and corn, and root vegetables like potatoes, turnips and sugar beet could all be transported in heavier loads, further and faster than ever before. Livestock could also be moved from farms to cattle markets in open wagons as long as the farmer could get his animals down to the local station where special animal pens had been erected. Takeley, Dunmow, Rayne and Braintree all had a cattle dock as part of their goods yards and these would become especially busy prior to market days at places like Bishops Stortford and Chelmsford where the wagons would transport pigs, sheep, cows and all manner of other livestock by rail. But mixing up both passenger and animal traffic could create unforeseen problem – especially if the animals got loose,  as can be seen from this report in the Chelmsford Chronicle from July 1887 demonstrates:

'On Tuesday afternoon a calf belonging to Mr Wisbey, of Thaxted, which had been brought to the railway station for transit, made its way into the old booking office and dashed through the window, breaking a pane of glass more than a quarter of an inch thick'.

Horses were transported on the railway from time to time in special wagons and a mishap while shunting caused one of the worst accidents on the railway. In January 1888 two horseboxes (containing three horses) were being shunted at Dunmow, when they suddenly rolled off down the gradient towards Felsted. They gathered speed and finally slammed into the approaching Braintree to Bishops Stortford passenger train killing two horses instantly and seriously injuring the third. The firemen from the passenger train sustained injuries as he leapt from the tender and several of the passengers were also hurt. The Chronicle reported it in great detail:

'Bradley, the guard, sustained a serious cut on the left temple, a young lady had her leg crushed, Mrs Smith and her daughter Mrs Robbins had their heads driven against the woodwork of their compartment and Mr Doubleday was thrown violently from side to side, his head coming into contact with the partition.'

Another major source of traffic at this and just about every other railway was coal. At a time when everything was coal-fired, from houses to businesses, and, of course, steam trains themselves, every Victorian railway station had a coal yard. Often run by the local coal merchant, a coal yard would supply local towns and villages with various different types of coal, depending on its use. I am just old enough to remember the coalman lumbering in with huge sacks of coal on his back (weighing 112 lbs each) and depositing them in my grandmother's coal bunker in her garden. She would then mix it with coke (like coal but cheaper to buy) which would make her open fire last longer. On the odd occasion that she had a little extra money then she would buy a bag or two of the more expensive Coalite or Anthracite and this would burn with much less smoke than normal coal.

*Dunmow Station in the early 1900s (SSPL)*

With so much coal being consumed by both homes and businesses the local coal yard at the railway station would always be a busy, bustling place with great mountains of jet-black coal, each one separated by walls made from old railway sleepers. When I was young coal was rapidly being replaced by oil and gas but back in the Victorian era it literally fired up the Industrial Revolution. No business could run without it. And for that reason the transport of coal from coal mines to factories, usually via the railway network, became vital to the prosperity of the country.

Goods, whether raw materials like coal or agricultural produce from farms, actually became the driving force behind the early railways. This growth of goods traffic was a real boost to the railways in their early years and certainly the Bishops Stortford to Braintree line benefited greatly from all sorts of non-passenger activity. However, even before the railways were to come under pressure from the growing road network, industrialisation would see the demand for local businesses like malt houses shrink. The trend was towards ever-bigger processing plants where mechanical innovations could improve the malting process, and sadly this was to be at the expense of the small producers. Dunmow Maltings finally closed its doors in the late 1940s and was consigned to brewing history. Today, many malt houses still exist either as private homes or are converted into flats or holiday homes and can always be spotted by their distinctive funnel-shaped roof vents which poke up skywards.

It is time to leave town now and so I cut through the back streets in an attempt to pick up the old railway. Of all the stations along the line, Dunmow is alone in having lost just about all traces of a railway. A bypass was built following the line of the track and a small business park occupies all the land where the station building once stood. There are only two indications that there was ever a railway here. Firstly, at the far end of New Street (where the bypass is crossed by a footbridge) is the unmarked spot where way back in 1864 a silver spade was used to cut the first sod of earth to mark the beginning of railway construction. And then as I walk out of town a street sign points out that I am now passing 'Station Road' and its long terrace of houses that would have once led to the booking office, goods yard, cattle pens and coal store. This break in the railway formation brought about by the building of the Dunmow bypass and industrial estate poses the only real problem that I have had in following the old railway. Up until now I have navigated the old track-bed without problem, even when crossing the M11 motorway; but trying to pick up the Flitch Way as I leave Dunmow has left me stumped.

*Original Dunmow signage can now be found at the East Anglian Railway Museum in Chappel and Wakes Colne*

The most notable feature of the railway as it leaves Dunmow has now vanished. The seven-arch brick viaduct which once crossed the Chelmer Valley was demolished in 1977 and today there is very little left of this once substantial structure other than two brick outcrops on either side of the valley. This physical gap in the railway does pose problems in picking up the route of the Flitch Way and without my trusty Ordnance Survey Map (which would have clearly outlined the old railway) I get just a little bit lost and spend the next 45 minutes crisscrossing several ploughed fields until finally I can see a tell-tale embankment in the distance. My only problem is that to get to it I have to cross a small river. I follow the riverbank in both directions in the hope of finding a bridge or some sort of crossing and then realise that I am just going to have to find a shallow spot and wade across. I will gloss over the finer points of my river crossing technique except to say that I finally made it back to the railway with an hour lost, two soaking wet feet and a lesson learned. That lesson being; when walking in future always stick to designated footpaths and always carry a good map.

Once I have climbed the embankment the footpath markings begin to reappear and I can now resume the second half of my walk. This spot in the Chelmer Valley is the ten-mile mark of the Bishops Stortford to Braintree Railway. In front of me is another eight miles of track-bed, several old stations and of course, more railway people.

# 7 A Ghost Station

The Great Eastern Railway (GER) was once called 'God's Excellent Railway' and that may have been true in the period between the two world wars, but the early years from 1862 onwards were anything but excellent. It inherited the legacy and practices of its predecessor, the Eastern Counties Railway and in doing so actually hampered the formation of a good and sustainable railway network for the future. In particular its preoccupation with stopping other railways from encroaching on its territory led to costly and time-consuming battles where new railways were proposed simply as a blocking tactic in the hope of frustrating one of their competitors. This fierce rivalry had two obvious outcomes.

*Crest of the Great Eastern Railway*

Firstly, a lot of time and money was spent on paying solicitors, buying up land, lodging plans and possibly going to the expense of pushing through a new act of parliament. And this was all done not in the interest of building a much-needed new railway but of hopefully <u>not</u> building a new railway and thereby protecting territory. Then secondly, if all else failed and they could not either buy up, pay-off or block the ambitions of a rival then a new railway would be built; probably in a sparsely populated, rural area. This new branch line would then have to be staffed and maintained alongside all the other stations and track and rolling stock on the GER network from an ever-dwindling pot of money. With a background like this it is no wonder that the GER almost went bankrupt in 1867 and new money had to be raised to keep the company afloat.

Seen from that point of view it is easy to understand why the Bishops Stortford to Braintree Railway was viewed as something of an 'unloved child' within the GER family. It was inherited from the final days of the Eastern Counties and having served its purpose of blocking the rival London and Bury St Edmunds Railway from getting access into East Anglia, it was all but forgotten by the GER. These spoiling and land-grabbing tactics were all too common and wide-spread in the early days of the railway network. If you ever venture into deepest Kent and find yourself in Royal Tunbridge Wells you will discover that this lovely small town had not one but two railway stations: Tunbridge Wells West and Tunbridge Wells Central. The rivalry between the South Eastern Railway and the London, Chatham and Dover Railway (both running lines into London) brought about a situation where in 1861 this small town had two completely independent railway lines, each competing for passenger and freight attention. This situation was brought about not by customer need but simply by the intense rivalry between the owners of the two companies. As Christian Wolmar put it in his excellent book, Fire and Steam: 'They were more intent on doing each other down, by competing on fares and building unnecessary lines which duplicated their rivals, rather than attempting to improve the quality of service for their passengers.'

Unfortunately this situation could be seen all over the country during and after the Railway Mania period and left a sprawling puzzle of a railway network that was hard to manage. At the Bishops Stortford to Braintree Railway there seems to have been a constant list of improvements requested and eventually undertaken. These included extending the goods sidings at Braintree in 1890, the rebuilding of several bridges to accommodate heavier locomotives in 1894 and further expansion at Rayne Station in 1901 to provide cattle pens and new platform buildings. In 1910 a new halt was built at Hockerill (just over a mile from Bishops Stortford) mainly for the use of the local golf club which used land on both sides of the railway, and this was to be the first of several new halts that were to be built on the line over the coming years. Yet many of these and numerous other improvements were a long time coming and they all added to the impression of a railway that was constantly in a state of catch-up.

The First World War brought many changes to the railways. From simply a practical point of view it didn't make sense for all the independent railways to continue competing against each other during wartime, especially when there would need to be coordination of things like troop movements and munitions delivery across the country. Central Government therefore took control of all railway companies from the outbreak of war. Along the Bishops Stortford branch line the pre-war timetables remained much the same, although the Sunday service was scrapped in 1917 due to the lack of coal, but extra goods services were introduced to carry food supplies into the cities. A very interesting article in the Essex Chronicle dated February 1916 gives a detailed report from the AGM of the Great Eastern Railway, which goes into great length to describe the effects of the war on the railway. Lord Claud Hamilton (chairman) stated that the GER: 'had run during the year 8,374 passenger and 3,634 goods trains exclusively for military purposes; this gave an extra 230 trains per week and 32 per day. The locomotive department had built four ambulance trains. As to the staff and the war, some 1,700 men rejoined the colours and by the end of September 1914 the number of their men serving was over 3,000, or ten per cent (of the workforce)'.

These figures give some idea as to the scale of the war effort from a railway perspective. In another interview dated 13 August 1915 with the then General Manger of the GER (Mr H W Thornton) the sheer number of train movements at Liverpool Street becomes apparent. He states that: 'With probably one exception, and that is St Lazare Station in Paris, there are more trains in and out of Liverpool Street than any other railway station in the world. From 6am until 9.30am there are 278 trains arriving and the number of passengers alighting during these three and an half hours is about 75,000. During the entire twenty-four hours there are almost 700 trains arriving at the station and about the same number departing.'

It is at this point that the name 'God's Excellent Railway' could quite rightly be given to the GER. Although it suffered huge damage due to the effects of the Great War, and for all its earlier dubious financial and business practices, the GER was now to go on to prove itself as not only an innovative railway but also one that could run an intensive steam service like no other. By providing cheap tickets on early morning trains, great swathes of North and East London were now opened up to commuters, and by perfecting the quick turn-around of the suburban steam services (a train could arrive, alight its passengers and then switch its engine; all within four and a half minutes) Liverpool Street Station ran the busiest and most intensive service of its day. At times 24 trains per hour were running over the same tracks; even the newly electrified railways in South London could not compete with the sheer volume of trains and people being moved by the GER.

A full Great Eastern Railway timetable from 1922 is quite something. It is A4 in size and runs to 174 densely packed pages. There were the intensive suburban services to places such as Tottenham, Stratford, Woolwich, Walthamstow, Enfield, Chingford, Hertford, Buntingford, Ongar and Broxbourne. Further afield trains were running to places like Chelmsford, Saffron Walden, Cambridge and Newmarket, and then out into East Anglia to Ipswich, Bury, Ely, Peterborough, Cambridge, Colchester, Norwich, Yarmouth, Kings Lynn and Lowestoft. Not only that but then there were the special services like Clacton Pullman Non-Stop Express, which for 28 shillings would take you first class (14 shillings for third class) from Liverpool Street to the coast in one hour and thirty-seven minutes; or the Continental Services running to Harwich where you could then pick up a boat to the Hook of Holland, Antwerp or Zebrugge.

If you wanted to venture to the seaside then you could hop on a train to all manner of places including: Southend-on-Sea, Wells, Walton-on-Naze, Frinton-on-Sea, Cromer or Sherringham and then there were the light railway services from Kelvedon to Tollesbury and from Elsenham to Thaxted. Finally the GER were running branch lines to places like Maldon, Brightlingsea, Stoke Ferry, Bartlow and, of course, - Braintree.

The 1922 timetable suggests a weekday service from Bishops Stortford to Braintree of seven trains, with the first service leaving Stortford at 8.58am. Of the returning six trains the final one leaves Braintree at 6.30pm and arrives at Stortford around 7.13pm. The journey time for the 18 mile branch line is around 43 minutes. For several reasons 1922 was to be a significant year on the Bishops Stortford to Braintree line.

## BISHOP'S STORTFORD. DUNMOW. BRAINTREE AND W

**WEEK DAYS.**

The table lists stations including: BISHOP'S STORTFORD (dep.), Takeley, Easton Lodge, Dunmow, Felstead, Rayne, Braintree and Bocking, Cressing, White Notley, WITHAM, Colchester, Ipswich, Chelmsford, LONDON (Liverpool St.).

And the return direction: LONDON (Liverpool St.) dep., Chelmsford, WITHAM, Ipswich, Colchester, Witham, White Notley, Cressing, Braintree and Bocking, Rayne, Felstead, Dunmow, Easton Lodge, Takeley, BISHOP'S STORTFORD arr.

Bishop's Stortford dep., Saffron Walden, Cambridge, Bishop's Stortford, Broxbourne & Hoddesdon arr., LONDON (Liverpool St.) arr.

Notes:
C  Calls when required to take up or set down. Passengers wishing to alight at these stations must inform Guard at preceding stopping station.
D  On Saturdays leaves Broxbourne 2.38 and arrives Bishop's Stortford 2.8 p.m.
E  Calls at Easton Lodge to set down passengers only.
FO  Fridays only.
NF  Not Fridays.
NS  Not Saturdays.
SO  Saturdays only.

T  From 10th to 22nd inclusive, runs
X  On Saturdays, 15th &
Z  Not after 16th Sept

For service between Witham and Maldon, see page 32.

*Part of the extensive GER timetable from 1922*

At the end of that year the GER decided to build two new halts along the line; one at Stane Street between Hockerill Halt and Takeley and another at Bannister Green, which was between Felsted and Rayne. All these ground-level halts were modest affairs with no buildings or shelter to speak of. There were no staff at these halts and tickets were issued on the train.

Halts were seen as cost-effective attempts to lure more passengers onto the railway with the minimum of over-heads and were very much a reaction to the newly arrived bus services, which had begun to spring up in local areas. In fact 1920 saw the first bus service begin running between Dunmow and Bishops Stortford and this would have been seen as a direct challenge to the railway, as for much of that journey the old Roman road called Stane Street runs directly parallel to the railway and could therefore compete with it mile for mile. And herein lies one of the fundamental problems with the railway network. Once track has been laid and stations built you are left with an inflexible form of transport. Stations cannot easily be moved if they prove to be in the wrong place and although extra stops (or halts) can be built, they still have to be along the railway formation that has already been established. If the growth of a town or village is away from the station, or worse still if the station is already situated away from a built-up area, then as soon as a bus or coach service offers several stopping points right in the middle of town, the railway is going to suffer.

It sounds obvious that a station should be situated in the middle of town, but for several reasons that may not be the case. Firstly, they could just grow in a direction away from the railway (perhaps towards a major road) until the station ends up sitting on one side of town or another. But quite often it is simply a question of building the railway so that it avoids steep gradients, hills and valleys. Crossing difficult terrain costs a lot of money and for a railway company where funds are low (as they were are the GER) then finding a cheaper route even at the expense of putting the railway right at the centre of the population might be preferable; especially as up until 1920 there was no effective competition to the railway. However, saving money by laying the track along easy terrain can be taken to extremes and a classic example of this is the Light Railway that ran from Elsenham to Thaxted in Essex.

Light railways were built as a cheaper alternative to the traditional 'heavy' railway in that the locomotives and carriages had a lower maximum weight and a restricted speed. To keep costs down they would avoid, as far as possible, any expensive earthworks, such as embankments and cuttings, and tunnels and bridges were kept to a minimum. The stations were also more likely to be constructed as halts, with few staff and little protection from bad weather. The Elsenham to Thaxted was one such light railway and it suffered from one, very big handicap: the Chelmer Valley. This railway was constructed as a six-mile branch line from the village of Elsenham, cutting across farmland on gentle gradients and stopping at the occasional halt before finally reaching the picturesque village of Thaxted. However, the final mile required the track to cross the deep depression of the Chelmer Valley. On a normal railway, a viaduct would have been constructed and the station would have probably been situated right in the village. But to save money Thaxted Station was built high up on the wrong side of the valley and nearly a mile away from where it needed to be.

Today it is a very pleasant, if hilly, walk that takes you from the location of the old station (much of which still exists by the way) and across the valley into Thaxted, but it is probably not one you would want to do every day. And certainly not if there was a brand new bus service that would pick you up and drop you off in the middle of the village. The Elsenham to Thaxted Light Railway finally closed in 1953 and so never came under the axe of the Beeching Cuts of the early 1960s. However, it does show that although a poorly sited railway station may survive when then is no effective competition, as soon as buses and coaches and cars become commonplace then its days are usually numbered.

The year 1922 was also to mark the end of one chapter in the history of our railways and the beginning of yet another. Out of the ashes of the First World War came the realisation that the railway network actually worked rather well under the hand of government control and that although it had ended up starved of funds and with its rolling stock in poor condition, the way ahead should really be approached with a more unified structure. Or as the 1921 Act of Parliament put it, 'the railways shall be formed into groups…and the principal railway companies in each group shall be amalgamated, and other companies absorbed in the manner provided by this Act'. This was to mean the end of The Great Eastern Railway along with over 100 other independent railway companies who would all end up amalgamated into just four regional companies, each one split along geographic lines.

From 1 January 1923 the United Kingdom saw the creation of four new railway companies: the Southern Railway (encompassing most of the southern counties of England but not the South-West region), the London, Midland and Scottish Railway (Central and Northern areas including parts of Scotland), the Great Western Railway (South-West and Wales) and the London and North East Railway (Eastern England and parts of Scotland). The London and North East Railway (or LNER as it became known) was the amalgamation of seven railway companies including such names as the Hull and Barnsley Railway, the Great Central Railway and the Great North of Scotland Railway. And it is into this new 'grouping' as it was called that the Great Eastern Railway finally ended up. In later years the old GER region was still to prove to be a valuable asset to the LNER as the goods traffic from East Anglia and the growing demand for sugar beet would push up revenues while other income was falling. But from 1923 the GER was gone in all but name. A company, which at one time employed over 30,000 people and ran trains over more than 1,000 miles of track, would now have to play its part in a much greater enterprise.

*Felsted Station House after recent renovation*

Today the Great Eastern Railway's legacy mainly exists in its buildings. The stations still stand as fine examples of Victorian architecture and where they have been restored with care (as at Rayne) they can survive as a living history of a bygone age. Liverpool Street Station and its old Great Eastern Hotel still shout out the name GER from many angles with embossed company initials and crests still easily seen high up on the buildings. And for those with eagle eyes even the old Eastern Counties Railway name and symbols can be found if you know where to look.

The GER with its early days of poor financial management and ruthless approach to dealing with its competitors had finally emerged as a pioneer of railway innovation, only to end up itself as just another casualty of railway integration. However, history has a funny way of repeating itself and it was not to be too long before the railways in the UK would go through yet more upheaval and reorganisation - not once but twice.

Day 2, 2pm

I have left behind the roar of planes coming in to land at Stansted Airport and the background hum of road traffic at Takeley, and the route of the old railway now takes on much more of a rural feel. The breaks in the hedgerow give glimpses of rolling farmland with the occasional Second World War pillbox partially concealed in a hedge and I am all too aware that I have lots of wildlife for company. In particular blackbirds, great tits, robins and woodpigeons seem to be happy to make a home in this disused railway embankment. I am also sharing the footpath with the occasional jogger and mountain-biker, splashing through the mud, as we exchange the customary 'good afternoon'. However, human contact is few and far between as I pass the small hamlet of Little Dunmow and follow the winding footpath for just under two miles as it brings me around to the front of another 1865-style railway station. At 11 ½ miles the railway now reaches Felsted.

The building stands empty and awaiting renovation, but I have been given permission to take a look around what could well be one of the last remaining stations of its kind. It stands as something of a time capsule and appears to be untouched since its final closure in 1964. Felsted is remarkably similar to other stations on the Bishops Stortford to Braintree Railway in that half of the building comprises a two-story living quarters, while the remainder is the ground floor booking office and waiting room. It is built from red brick with the hallmark Georgian sash windows and stone surrounds. The station is still decked out in the colours of the LNER with the window frames painted cream while the booking office door is mid-green.

*Felsted Station in the days of the GER (Lens of Sutton)*

Before I venture into the building I take a look around the extensive garden, which backs onto the platform. Once well-tended, this garden must be 40ft long by 40ft wide and contains splashes of colour from roses and foxgloves that have started to run wild. There is a brick-built outhouse and several sheds, one of which looks to be an old railway freight wagon with its wheels removed; now cobwebbed and gently rotting after many years of heavy rain and summer sun. Today it may seem strange to think that a railway station garden would have been all that important, but back in the days of steam, they were a source of great pride. Many railway companies held competitions each year to award prizes for the best-kept stations in each region and Essex Newsman newspaper from September 1926 reported that those awarded 'first class' distinction (and a prize of £7 and

6 shillings) included Bartlow and White Notley. There is no mention of any of the Bishops Stortford to Braintree stations but Takeley does get a mention in the 'highly commended' category. Actually, the tiny station of White Notley (still open and situated between Braintree and Witham) took first place for over seven years running in the 1920s, which suggests that the staff there must have been extraordinarily green-fingered considering the station is little bigger than your average halt.

*Platform view, early 1900s (Lens of Sutton)*

Just as countless passengers would have done before me, I enter the station through the booking office door. The ladies' waiting room and ticket office are on the right and the platform straight ahead, while on the left is a small door that leads to the stationmaster's accommodation. Although the furniture has all been long since removed, the glass ticket hatch and classic stable door (where you could open the top or bottom half independently) are still here. All around there is peeling green and cream paintwork and inside the ticket office the walls retain their original GER chocolate brown colouring. The booking office and waiting room still have their open fireplaces, which would have provided a very warm refuge for passengers waiting for a train on a cold winter's day, while a very rusty cast-iron safe sits heavily on the floor of the ticket office where it would look after the daily takings at the station. Out on the platform, nature has reclaimed the trackside area and a thick covering of trees and bushes prevents me from even attempting to drop down to where the track would have been. There is no hint of the old signal box, goods siding or the coal yard, but who knows, they may still exist, hidden somewhere behind the dense thicket of weeds and foliage. The only piece of railway furniture that I can find is a lonely sack-barrow that sits patiently on the platform as if waiting to collect its last parcel.

The Felsted Station of the mid 1920s was a very different place. As well as the additional goods loop and coal yard, the station benefited from the opening of a sugar beet processing plant close to the railway, which greatly increased traffic on the line. A dedicated sidings of up to seven tracks was built to the south of the station and once the factory opened in 1926, Felsted handled over 42,000 tons of sugar beet that year. By the standards of the Bishops Stortford to Braintree Railway, Felsted became a busy station! The staff of six included the stationmaster, signalman, booking clerk and porters. In particular the role of the signalman became very important at Felsted as what had become a busy mix of goods traffic had also to be efficiently woven in and out of the regular passenger traffic. The points controlling the main line, passing loop and the sugar beet sidings were all under the control of one signalman. And right up until the signal box finally closed at Felsted in 1967, the signalman was Horace Hicks.

Horace started working on the railways in 1945 when he was just 16 years old, as a porter at Dunmow Station. From there he moved on to become signalman at Felsted until its closure in 1964, and then he spent another 23 years at Braintree Station. In all Horace worked on the railway for over 46 years and was clearly a railway man through and through. At his retirement in 1991 it was obvious that Horace preferred the days of steam on the railways when he said: "It was more of a railway back then – nowadays it is more like a Meccano set".

Once he had retired Horace and his wife stayed on as tenants at Felsted Station with the public part of the building boarded up, while they lived in the old stationmaster's house and they had use of the large garden. Living a 'railway life', even after retirement, would have been quite common-place for people of Horace's generation. Many came from railway families where their fathers and even grandfathers may have worked on either the stations or tracks or trains of the early railways. And as we saw with Madeline Scraggs (who lives at Easton Lodge) that desire to live on or close to a railway never really goes away.

Sadly, Horace Hicks died in 2012 and this has led to the old station being put up for sale. Clearly the building requires refurbishment but I do hope that whoever buys Felsted Station will renovate it with a degree of respect for its original design and character. These old 1865-style stations are not only part of our industrial history, they are also beauti-fully designed Georgian buildings and they deserve to be looked after and protected.

# 8 A Second Life

The old cast-iron bridge that used to take the railway away from Felsted and on towards Rayne and Braintree has now been removed leaving only the brick side-supports still standing, and this means that I have to drop down from the old station and cross the road to pick up the footpath on the other side. And it is at this point, as I cross this road in the middle of nowhere, it occurs to me that Felsted Station is actually in the wrong place.

Felsted village is probably a half-mile walk from where I am standing and even though a new housing estate has recently been built close by, there would only have been a smattering of homes here when the railway was in existence. With much of the land between here and the village quite hilly the railway was built to the north of the population on relatively flat terrain, and this eventually put the railway at a distinct disadvantage. The situation may not be as bad as at Thaxted but the honest truth is that Felsted Station was never put in a convenient place for people in the village.

*Felsted village has changed little over the years*

Felsted is as near-perfect example of a traditional East Anglian village as you could wish to find. It sits in rolling countryside close to the River Chelmer and is dominated by the Norman built Holy Cross Church on Station Road. From here, traditional timber-framed houses spread out along the meandering side streets and are interspersed with local shops and the occasional pub. In typical East Anglian style there is a mixture of medieval and Tudor buildings here with white painted houses, exposed beams and thatched roofs dotted around the village. Would it have stayed this way if the railway had still been around today? I doubt it very much. A railway may not only bring new life to a location, it can also change it beyond recognition and it is quite possible that the loss of its railway has helped to keep Felsted, and countless other small villages up and down the country, unchanged and unspoilt.

The rural nature of this area is reflected in the surveys of the time where between 1871 and 1931 the population of Felsted consistently stayed at around 2,000. Even by 1961 the population was still only 2,056. The same is also true of the other stations on the line, as neither Takeley, Dunmow or Rayne had any significant rise in population during the time that the railway was present. Only at the towns of Bishops Stortford and Braintree did population numbers take off. Between 1871 and 1961 Bishops Stortford went from 6,250 inhabitants to 18,342, while Braintree jumped from 4,790 to 20,600. Of those two, Bishops Stortford benefited from being on the main line into London and although Braintree was on the Dunmow branch it also had another line running via Witham to Liverpool Street. These factors helped turn both towns into the large conurbations that they are today.

There is a clear indication here that the coming of the railways to this area did not have any noticeable effect on the number of people either living or working in the more remote and rural parts of north Essex. But the rise and fall of branch line Britain wasn't just a story of a failure to attract enough passengers onto the railways. There were other factors at play in the decline of the rural lines and it wasn't until a myriad of other problems had surfaced that the writing was truly on the wall for the Bishops Stortford to Braintree Railway, as well as many other lines just like it.

*The view from the old railway across fields to Felsted*

The fortunes of the LNER can roughly be divided into two parts. First, there is the period from its birth, in 1923, until 1933; and then from 1934 until the outbreak of the Second World War in 1939. These two periods show both the best and the worst of the railways. There were to be golden days, where steam engines would go on reach their peak in terms of technological achievement, and there were to be darker times when the railways were to be challenged by competition in a way that they would find hard to match.

Firstly, freight started making what was to be an inexorable move away from the railways and onto the road – and the transport of coal took the first hit. The handling of coal on the LNER dropped from 102 million tonnes in 1923 to just 87 million by 1925 and in addition to this the cost of buying coal (to run steam engines) had leapt by 80 per cent since the end of the First World War. Then there were crippling wage demands from the unions, which if implemented would cost the company an additional £14 million every year. The LNER was not alone in having to grapple with these problems. Indeed, every railway company was suffering at a time when the country as a whole was in the grip of the depression that emerged from aftermath of the war. But with its high dependence on goods traffic, the LNER could expect to be hit harder that some others.

However, one ray of hope came from the former GER region of East Anglia (including Felsted) as the transport of goods, and in particular sugar beet, rose by 20 per cent, giving a much-needed boost to the depleted coffers of the LNER.

But a far greater problem arose with the General Strike of 1926 in which the railways were shut for seven long days in May of that year. The strike was called by the TUC in support of coal miners who had seen their pay reduced partly due to an influx of cheap coal from abroad. The railway workers (to the surprise of the management) supported the strike and the whole of the railway network came to a halt. Although the General Strike eventually came to an end, the miners' strike was to continue well into the autumn and this had the effect of seriously depleting the coal stocks to such an extent that many train services had to be cancelled. All of these factors had a drastic effect on the fortunes of the LNER and one look at their income for that period paints a bleak picture. In their first year of operation the income at the LNER was £14 million, in 1924 it was less that £12 million and by 1925 it had dropped again to just over £10 million. Finally, in 1926 (the year of the General Strike) it had plummeted to only £4.5 million. So difficult was the situation on the railway that by mutual agreement between the management and the unions the entire staff agreed a temporary pay cut of 3.5 per cent. At the same time there were several rounds of cost-cutting and eventually the company managed to regain control of its finances; by the end of 1931 a total of just over £4 million had been saved.

The General Strike and its long felt after-effects did mark something of a turning point for the railways. In particular, the move away from transporting goods and freight from rail and onto road seemed to speed up. And although the drift to road transport started in the early 1920s, the strike of 1926 changed a lot of attitudes. It is around this time that train passengers also started to see viable alternatives to the railway and in particular the growth of car and bus traffic started to make its impact felt. There is no more obvious example of this than the official passenger numbers themselves. In 1923 the total number of passengers that went through Takeley and Rayne stations were 13,700 and 14,000 respectively, but in 1928 those numbers had dropped to 11,100 and 9,800. That is a dramatic shift in just five years and it was a trend that was to continue downwards as more people started to own cars, and the provision of frequent and convenient bus and coach services became more commonplace. However, this downward trend was to be arrested for a short period at least. And it happened to coincide with perhaps the greatest period in the history of the London and North East Railway.

If the period 1923 to 1933 was a wretched, depressed time for the railways then what was to follow was anything but. A spirit of innovation and competition between the big four companies saw newer and faster trains introduced, and there was even to be an increase in freight traffic. In particular the fierce rivalry between the London Midland and Scottish

Railway (LMS) and the LNER over the lines running from London to the North of England and into Scotland gave rise to some of the most iconic steam engines ever. New stream-lined engines like the Coronation Scot (LMS) and the Mallard (LNER) fought to bring down the non-stop London to Scotland times and found ever more ingenious ways to do so. To provide a non-stop service to Scotland meant a journey of nearly 400 miles without the customary stop to take on water. To get around this problem the LMS intro-duced water troughs. These were narrow troughs, several hundred yards in length, placed between the running rails and filled with water. A special scoop was then fitted to the engine and would be lowered by the fireman at the correct point on the track, water would be funnelled up into the tank on the engine, and then the scoop raised again as the end of the trough was reached. This was a clever idea first thought of in the 1860s that would prove invaluable in what was to be coined 'The Race to the North'.

For their part the LNER realised that to run a non-stop service for 400 miles would require more than one train crew, and so they developed the corridor-tender. This allowed the train crew to be changed mid-journey when the relief crew (who were seated in the first passenger coach) would walk through a small corridor, no more than 18 inches wide, that had been built into one side of the coal tender. They would then take over from the original driver and fireman, who would then go off-duty via the corridor-tender and back into the passenger coach. Such innovations allowed the railway companies to shave vital minutes off the London to Scotland journey time and so give them a new advantage over their competition. However, the biggest advantage of all was to be had through one thing. Speed.

The famous locomotive The Flying Scotsman was the first steam engine to reach 100mph and in doing so it helped bring down the London to Scotland journey time. In 1928 the non-stop Kings Cross to Edinburgh express would take around 8 hours, 15 minutes to cover 393 miles. However, by 1938 advances in engine technology had reduced that to 7 hours, 20 minutes. More powerful, streamlined engines working with the innovations such as water troughs and tender-coaches had brought the capabilities of humble steam engine close to its peak.

That moment was probably reached on 3 July 1938 when on a section of straight track near the village of Essendine in Lincolnshire the streamlined LNER steam locomotive called Mallard achieved a world speed record of 126mph. That speed, a record still held to this day, was never to be repeated in normal passenger service, but the significance of what Mallard, and by implication the LNER, had achieved was to go down in history as one of the greatest technological advances ever. The Mallard was to eventually head the non-stop 'Elizabethan' service from Kings Cross to Edinburgh, which reduced the London to Scotland journey time to a mere 6 hours, 30 minutes. Bearing in mind that in 1862 the forerunners of the Flying Scotsman were taking over ten hours to complete the same journey, the steam engine had indeed come a long way.

The following year, 1939, was to be a defining one for both the railways and the whole country. Within a matter of months Europe was at war and all the railway companies would be pitched into the war effort. Their identities would be taken away and just as in the First World War, central government control would once again be exerted over all aspects of the network. The days of Grouping, the Big Four and of the London and North East Railway, London, Midland and Scottish Railway, Great Western Railway and Southern Railway, were all but over.

Sadly, most humble branch lines such as the Bishops Stortford to Braintree would never see any real benefit from
the achievements of the mainline railways. No Mallard or
A1 engine would ever clatter over the points at Felsted or
Rayne and the words 'high-speed' or 'non-stop' would never
be uttered in the waiting room at Takeley. The nearest to
excitement that this line would ever encounter would be the
occasional seaside excursion heading to Clacton. But going
to war was a different matter. At a time of war all railways
can be of great assistance to the country; whether that is
with the movement of food, munitions or people. And also
at a time of war railways become a target for enemy attack. A
railway line can be easily seen from the air, it can be bombed
or machine gunned, and it can be followed. Just like the
River Thames was used as a way of navigating bombers to
target London, so a railway track acts in much the same way.
Both mainline and branch line railways had their part to
play in the theatre of war.

*A walker heads out along the Flitch Way*

A major role for all the railways during the war was to be the movement of people, both civilian and military. The evacuation of thousands of children away from the danger of air raids in the city and into the relative safety of the countryside was a monumental task. And it was a task that only the railways could achieve. By the end of 1939 it was estimated that over 137,000 children had been evacuated to the East Anglian region alone. Many of these would have left Liverpool Street Station on special trains heading for Norfolk, Suffolk or Essex destinations and would end up spread around towns and villages. In some places this was to have a significant increase to population numbers. For example, 2,700 people were evacuated to Bishops Stortford, which meant that by July of 1940 the population of the town had grown by 50 per cent within the space of six months.

Military personnel also travelled all over the country using the railway network to get to and from their barracks and bases. In particular East Anglia (being close to the European mainland) had a large number of air bases dotted around every county, from where bomber and fighter aircraft could engage the enemy. At the height of the war there were 111 airbases in East Anglia, of which 13 were in Essex. They all required air crew and support staff. For many of these servicemen, Bishops Stortford Station was a popular stopping-off point as they made their way to airfields like Easton Lodge or Stansted.

This military activity meant that peaceful, rural East Anglia was anything but during the war and actually ended up as something of a prime target for enemy bombers. All of the 111 air bases could expect to come under aerial attack, during which munitions could easily be dropped off-target and hit civilian areas. The air bases at both Stansted and Easton Lodge were supplied with munitions via the railway and this made it another important target for German bombers.

But the railways were not alone in being at risk. Towns and industrial areas were easy targets, and both Braintree and Bishops Stortford were hit numerous times. In February 1941, three people were killed in Braintree when a stick of bombs were dropped on the town completely demolishing several buildings including the local Lloyds Bank. In 1940 local records show that at least 20 bombs were dropped in Bishops Stortford. And the danger from the air was not just confined to the towns. Throughout the war at least 12 bombs were dropped in and around the villages of Little Dunmow and Felsted and 12 V1 rockets (or Doodlebugs) exploded in the area. One record shows that a young lady called Joyce Stone, from Oxney Villas in Felsted, recalls being thrown in a ditch at the bottom of the garden by her brother as a V1 came down nearby. The V1 was a notoriously indiscriminate weapon and once launched would simply fly until its fuel ran out, when it would then plummet to earth.

Small villages like Felsted were never direct targets of enemy attack but that didn't stop them being hit on numerous occasions, usually as the result of either a bomber missing the intended target, indiscriminate munitions (as with the V1) or if the plane came under heavy anti-aircraft fire from the ground then the crew might decide to simply open the bomb doors and dump their munitions as fast as possible and return to base.

Walking along the route of the old railway today it is hard to imagine the upheaval that the Second World War brought to this area. The influx of evacuees into towns and villages, the coming and going of hundreds, if not thousands, of servicemen, the altered timetables with munition trains and ambulance trains, and then the dark days of the German bombing campaign. Considering the turmoil that the war brought to every corner of the country, you would think that it would have left more of a scar on the landscape of today.

But in fact there are not many wartime relics left behind for us to wonder at. RAF Stansted has been completely rebuilt and enlarged to become the fourth largest UK airport, while the old American airbase at Easton Lodge was demolished long ago. However, just a few miles back along the railway I do remember seeing something as I looked out across the open farmland between Dunmow and Felsted. It is a remnant of World War Two that is hiding in plain sight, partly hidden by an overgrown hedge. In fact, there is more than one, and once you know what to look for and where to look – you begin to see them everywhere. The pillbox.

*The old railway bridge near Felsted looks as good as new*

Second World War pillboxes were reinforced concrete fortifications, which were built in 1940 to form a last line of defence against a land invasion. Typical of many pillboxes, the ones that run here alongside the River Chelmer are either square, or six sided, about five feet high and have bullet-proof walls that are at least a foot thick. Each pillbox could hold six to eight soldiers who could then fire small arms, rifles and machine guns through the narrow, windowless slits that were built into each wall. They were designed to frustrate and hold back any attack that came from the east in the event of a seaborne invasion through the eastern counties, and hopefully allow enough time for crucial reinforcements to arrive. Pillboxes, a vitally important part of the war effort, were not put randomly across the countryside but actually followed a defensive line to protect important industrial areas and cities. They often took advantage of natural obstacles like rivers and steep banks and were sometimes fortified with tank traps and emplacements for heavy artillery. The line that cuts through Essex and passes Dunmow was called the General Headquarters Line (GHQ) and was the longest defensive line in the UK, stretching all the way from Yorkshire to Kent, then turning west through Sussex and on towards Bristol.

Over 28,000 pillboxes were built across the country in 1940 and of these possibly 1,000 are still standing. Within Essex, 81 formed the GHQ line that ran from Newport, past Saffron Walden, Dunmow, Chelmsford and Basildon to finally reach the Thames Estuary at Pitsea. And although some of these have been dug up and destroyed, many do still exist, often in very good condition. It is this GHQ line of pillboxes that pass Dunmow and the old railway on their way south towards Chelmsford, and a number of them can still be seen to this day; sitting rather forlornly in farmers' fields, silent witnesses to a battle that thankfully never came.

Day 2, 3pm

With the old station at Felsted far behind me it is time to embark on the most peaceful and beautiful part of my journey along this old railway, where the steeple of Felsted Church can just be made out far over to the right, peeping out above trees in the distance. This stretch of the Flitch Way will eventually take me to Rayne Station and cuts through nearly four miles of rolling countryside. This early part of the walk benefits from the railway being built on an embankment from where I get fine views of the surrounding farmland, and any roads crossing the footpath must do so by passing underneath the railway. One such bridge is at Mill Lane, near Felsted and considering it was built in 1894, this iron girder bridge is remarkably well preserved and seems to have benefited from a recent coat of black gloss paint. In all there are 22 bridges that still remain on the Bishops Stortford to Braintree Railway and although some are small river crossings, others are large structures that either carry the railway above a public road or alternatively carry a road over the top of the railway. They can be roughly divided into two types; either of the brick arch or iron girder style of construction and for every year that passes they come under ever-greater threat of decay and demolition. A brick bridge will over time begin to lose its mortar and as that comes away so individual bricks then become loose, and if left in that state the structure will start to weaken. Once they start to crumble and become unsafe the question of what to do about them will probably fall to the local county council, and we can only hope that they will restore them sensitively and with respect to their original design.

The big fear will always be that to save money a bridge may be demolished and a permanent footpath diversion put in place, thereby both interrupting the course of the Flitch Way and also wrecking a valuable piece of Victorian architecture. I know it is not that easy to get excited over a bridge. A building or station perhaps, but a bridge? However, one of the great things about this old railway is that, with the exception of a few gaps in the line, you can still walk along most of the old track-bed. But if the bridges were slowly dismantled and the footpath re-routed, it becomes more of an obstacle course than a country walk.

Perhaps the answer lies in some sort of preservation order or 'listing' of all of these bridges before it is too late. Just as many other Victorian structures are only now receiving preservation orders, it must surely be possible to do the same along parts of the Flitch Way. Without some form of protection there has to be the real possibility that not just these bridges, but also others all over the country, will eventually be deemed to be unsafe and we could lose them forever. Another bit of our industrial heritage gone – and we won't get them back.

*The restored halt at Bannister Green*

However, as I don't want to labour the point and come across as some sort of anorak regarding bridges, it is probably time to move on to a structure that has thankfully been brought back into use, many years after its closure.

Up ahead, at just over the 13-mile point of the railway, sits the small but perfectly restored halt at Bannister Green. It is almost identical to Stane Street Halt, near Takeley and it boasts the same basic design of a ground level clinker base, nameboard and train timetable. And that's about it.

*Then and now: above from the early 1950s (DT Towe) and below as it looks today*

When the halt was operational there would have been the addition of a single oil lamp to provide lighting in the late evening or early morning, but this would have been kept alight and filled with oil by staff from the nearly Rayne or Felsted Stations as Bannister Green had no staff of its own. With no buildings or shelter at the halt, and very few houses nearby, Bannister Green must have been one of the loneliest places to wait for a train on the whole branch line. Since the day it opened in December 1922 this halt served a very sparse parish, sited between the small villages of Felsted and Rayne, and as an attempt to lure more people onto the railway it was never going to be able to compete with local buses. The halt finally closed in 1952 and over the years was reclaimed by nature until the Friends of the Flitch Way decided to rebuild both Bannister Green and Stane Street Halts in 2011. And the rest, as they say, is history.

*The unique habitat of Dunmow Cutting*

Since their formation in 2004 the Friends of the Flitch Way have provided something unique to this old railway. Headed by their determined chairman, Stan Davies, this small group of volunteers takes work parties out onto the footpath twice a week where they do all they can to conserve the natural habitat along the track-bed. It could be anything from coppicing trees to cutting back hedgerows to clearing ditches. They have also cut back overhanging trees, allowing sunlight to breakthrough and reach the footpath once again. All of this is done with the aim of encouraging more animal and plant life back to the railway.

Carl Blamire, one of the Friends and a keen butterfly enthusiast, recently told me: "Old railway lines are really the motorways of the insect world. By opening up the canopy, flora can return and this brings with them insects and birds."

It certainly seems to have worked. Dragonflies are now commonplace along the railway and in the spring and summer you may well see butterflies like the Common Blue, Meadow Brown or the Essex Skipper, especially if you venture up to Dunmow Cutting, where the chalky soil and meadow-like appearance of the footpath provide a haven for all sorts of plants and insects. I have even heard a rumour that there are orchids flowering in the cutting most summers. But it is not just the return of nature that the Friends of the Flitch Way have managed to achieve along this disused railway. They are also keen to keep the history of this old branch line alive by bringing back some of its old industrial heritage as well. The rebuilding of both Stane Street and Bannister Green Halts has only been possible through the determination and hard work of the Friends. By studying old photographs of the halts they have managed to build them from scratch with a striking similarity to the original constructions. And not content with that, they have now embarked on an even greater challenge. They are now bringing an original railway carriage to Rayne Station where they will mount it onto a small section of reclaimed track, right next to the platform. The carriage will house a small museum that is dedicated to telling the story of the

Bishops Stortford to Braintree Railway.

As Stan Davies (chairman of the Friends) tells me: "Getting a carriage is something we have wanted to do for quite some time. It will bring more people to the country park – not just visiting the carriage but they will then see the whole Flitch Way as well."

Once the railway had closed there were two key things that have happened to keep it from just becoming an overgrown mess. Firstly, Essex County Council had the foresight to turn the entire length of the old track into a country park, thereby protecting it from building work. But just as importantly, the Friends of the Flitch Way along with the Essex County Rangers have done all they can to manage this wonderful footpath by carefully working to both encourage nature to return to it while at the same time opening it up for the public to enjoy.

With local authorities up and down the country cutting back spending on what they call 'non-essential' services such as green spaces and country parks, the work of voluntary groups like the Friends of the Flitch Way is going to become more important than ever. They are going to be the front line in protecting some of the hidden treasures of the countryside and they are going to need our help to do that. So, if you are taking a walk along the Flitch Way one day and you happen to meet up with some of the Friends, dressed in their dark green clothing, as they go about their work, please stop and give them a word or two of encouragement. I am sure they would appreciate that. And if you want to get more involved, the Friends are a registered charity and have an AGM each year where you can hear about their current work plus their plans for the future.

I very much doubt that back in 2004 the Friends ever envisaged that they could achieve quite as much as they have done to date. Today the Flitch Way is a unique country park, 15 miles in length, which has also managed to keep alive its railway history. All of this has only been possible through the hard work and dedication of a small group of volunteers who give both time and energy to keeping this landscape open for all to enjoy. For that we should all be very grateful.

*The wetlands area called the Boardwalk near Dunmow*

# 9 Railway People

Of all the people who have appeared in the pages of this book, none more typifies the 'railway life' than Jim Warner. Jim was born into a railway family in 1890 at the crossing-keeper's cottage in Haughley, Suffolk. His father was a platelayer on the railway and his mother was a crossing-keeper, and so it was probably no surprise that Jim was to follow this tradition when in 1906 (aged just 16) he began his employment with the Great Eastern Railway; working a 12-hour day, six days a week, as a porter at Rayne Station. This was to be the start of a long career on the railways that was to last over 50 years and which would eventually see him working through various jobs at Rayne, culminating in his promotion to stationmaster. In Cambridge in 1958 he was presented with a gold pocket-watch in recognition for his long dedication to the railway. Even though the passenger service had ceased on the line, Jim was still kept busy by the freight traffic, which was to run on the Bishops Stortford to Braintree Railway for several more years. Sadly, doing his usual morning rounds at the station on Christmas Day 1962, Jim Warner was taken ill, collapsed and died. So, in a way he never really left the railway.

Jim was born, lived, worked and died a railway man. Or, as his granddaughter movingly puts it: "Grandad was born by the railway, lived his whole life on the railway, finally falling asleep by the railway." In all, Jim Warner and his close family worked a staggering 400 years on the railways.

This idea of coming from a railway family and then working your whole life on the railways was commonplace in the late 19th and early 20th centuries, where handing down knowledge and experience through families was almost expected. It also cannot be coincidence that both Madeline Scraggs (at Easton Lodge) and Horace Hicks (at Felsted) remained living on railway property long after their retirement. It is as if they still felt an invisible bond with the railway and all that it had meant to them over the years. It never let go of them, always pulling them back.

Part of the reason is that despite all the hard and sometimes dangerous nature of railway work, the early railway companies were often seen as good employers, with many of them (including the financially precarious Great Eastern Railway) providing sick pay and pension entitlements to their staff.

*Rayne Station 2016*

Working on a railway provided a relatively secure job and for those who were dependable and worked hard there was the possibility of career progression. A station such as Rayne would have had a staff of seven during its busiest times and these would range from the lowly goods porter, through booking clerk and signalman, all the way up to stationmaster. And this was just at the smaller branch line stations. Larger, mainline stations would have an even greater number of staff and this meant that there were all sorts of jobs to be had on the railway.

On the trains themselves there were drivers, firemen and

guards, while the stations needed the staff mentioned above. Meanwhile all level crossings required crossing-keepers to work the gates and to look after the track required plate-layers, foremen and labourers. Another benefit of working on a railway was the possibility of accommodation for staff. The stationmaster and his family could live on-site at most stations, including all the ones on the Bishops Stortford to Braintree Railway, and all over the country what became known as railway cottages were built close to local stations, allowing staff to live near to their place of work. It wasn't just the material benefits of working on a railway that many people came to appreciate; railways provided a structure to the lives of the people that worked on it, and that could come through something as simple as the wearing of a uniform or of understanding your place in the strict hierarchy, and with it the possibility to work hard and move up through the ranks.

*Rayne under the GER in the early 1900s (Lens of Sutton)*

For many people the order, discipline and structure of working for a railway company was something that they actively enjoyed and, outside of working for one of the armed forces, was something they were unlikely to encounter else-where. These unique qualities of working on the railway gave many employees a deep affection for their work and their working lives, and it helped create a bond that even in retirement would be hard to break.

Day 2, 5pm

Another two miles of good walking along the old railway now brings me to the best-preserved and most authentic looking station on this old branch line. At just under the 16-mile point I reach the home and workplace of former stationmaster, Jim Warner. This is Rayne Station.

The village of Rayne was, and still is, a small settlement, just a couple of miles west of Braintree. Its railway station is positioned just a few hundred yards from the High Street and therefore, unlike some other stations (such as Felsted), there is no half-mile walk for weary passengers. Only 401 people lived in Rayne just after the railway arrived in 1871 and this rose to 760 by 1961. Today, although that number has grown to around 3,000 residents, the village has still managed to retain its small community atmosphere, partly helped by the construction of the nearby A120 bypass, which has dramatically reduced vehicle numbers along its quiet High Street. From here, a short walk down Station Road brings visitors to the old station itself.

The station buildings follow almost exactly the same design and layout as Takeley Station and if you stand on the old track-bed and look up, you will find the two-story accommodation block on the left with the booking office and porter's room to the right. Also to the right would have been the goods sidings, cattle pens and coal yard. Finally, sitting opposite the far end of the platform was the signal box. Sadly all of these have been dismantled and we are today left with only the main stations buildings and the platform. But what does remain must surely be one of the best-preserved examples of a Victorian branch line railway station anywhere.

Rayne Station closed to passengers in 1952 but continued to remain open until freight traffic on the line was withdrawn in 1964. The station quickly fell into disrepair with a badly leaking roof, broken windows and decaying woodwork. Then, after much local pressure, Essex County Council decided to renovate the building with the aim of not just making good the dilapidated structure but to actually return it to its former glory. With the help of local volunteers the roof was fixed, brickwork repointed and most of the rotting woodwork was replaced. Even the cream and green colours of the London and North East Railway were returned to the doors and window-frames. Finally, with the platform refurbished, restored to its full length, and with a new station name-board the last of the great 1865 stations had finally got its pride back.

The newly renovated Rayne Station opened in April 1995 with a café and small museum situated inside the old booking office and waiting room; slowly but surely word spread and people came to visit. Today, the station is bustling with walkers, runners and cyclists stopping off from their excursion to eat and drink at the café. The station has become a meeting point for all sorts of people and it is a very rare day to find yourself alone on the platform. The recent addition of the old British Railways coach at the far end of the platform has given people another reason to visit the old station and the museum has been moved out of the booking office and now occupies most of the old carriage.

Walking off the platform, through the heavy green door and into the waiting room is still like stepping back in time. On the right is the booking office with its old stable door and ticket hatch, but instead of selling tickets they now sell all manner of teas, coffees and pastries. The waiting room itself is resplendent in LNER green and cream paintwork and to my left, taking pride of place on this chilly autumn day, is the original open fireplace with a fire roaring away, surrounded by assorted café-dwellers. Some, judging by the splashes of mud on their legs, are cyclists; while others just seem to be enjoying piece of cake and a chat in the slightly surreal but very comfortable surroundings of what could almost be 1924.

Brenda Allard is sitting with her husband Malcolm at one of the small tables close to the fire, and she has a very special connection to Rayne Station. Brenda is the granddaughter of the old stationmaster, Jim Warner and spent much of her childhood exploring the station in the 1940s and 50s. Today, Brenda and Malcolm live a few miles away in Braintree. I ask Brenda what life was like in the 'private' part of the station where her grandfather lived?

*An old railway carriage now doubles as a museum*

"All of the rooms had high ceilings and many of the rooms had open fires. The ground floor had a medium-size kitchen, a sitting room, hall and stairway; and there was another room where the best of everything was kept – but never used! Upstairs had at least three spacious bedrooms, two of which gave very clear views of the platform and signal box. There was also a separate brick-built washhouse which contained a large copper (for boiling water) a mangle and a tin bath."

The brick washhouse is identical to the ones at Takeley and Felsted and is an indication that although the building had good-sized rooms it was also very basic in other ways. In fact, up until the late 1950s Rayne Station had no mains electricity, gas or water. I asked Brenda if this made life hard for the family.

"Yes, the long, dark nights of winter meant extra paraffin lamps and lanterns were needed", she said. "Lamps in the waiting room and ticket office had to be lit, plus the lamps along the platform. A good supply of logs, paraffin and candles made sure we had heat and light during the cold, dark times of winter."

I also wondered how they managed without water?

"Well, all the water at Rayne had to be hand-pumped," Brenda said, "The water was pumped out of the ground to a large storage tank which was situated above the gents toilets! From here a tap ran into a butler sink in the kitchen of the station house. When the supply in the tank ran out then it was time for Grandad to use the hand-pump to top up the water supply again."

All of this sounds quite grim in these days where we expect not only hot water and electricity at the turn of a tap or the flick of a switch, but also instant central heating. However, in years gone by such things as pumping water, using a mangle and cleaning out the ashes before you could light a fire were all just a part of everyday life. And as children we sometime forget the harsher side of life and remember instead the excitement and fun of every new adventure. I asked Brenda about the fun she had a Rayne Station.

"Before I started school I can remember the Sunday walks from the stationmaster's house. I knew that a whole new adventure was just behind the door at the end of the hallway. This was the door where the station house finished and the railway station started."

And did she ever visit the old signal box, opposite the platform?

"Yes I did, but to get to the signal box you had to climb down from the platform by placing your foot in a foot-hole, halfway down the platform wall and lowering yourself onto the line. But grandad told me that until I was big enough to reach it by myself I couldn't go to the signal box. Well, after many failed attempts I did it! I climbed down from the platform, up the wooden steps and into the signal box. I watched my grandad work the signal and points, and soon after a train appeared, billowing smoke."

Back in the days of semaphore signals every station would have its own signal box, working the points not only for the regular passenger trains but also to handle the goods traffic being shunted in and out of the goods yard. However, over time signalling gradually became more centralised until there was no longer a need for individual boxes at each station. Slowly but surely they were phased out.

I ask Brenda what else she got up to on her visits to Rayne?

"After Sunday dinner I always looked forward to walks along the line with my grandad. It was only possible to walk the tracks on a Sunday as that was the only day of the week that trains did not run, and my grandad used to walk from sleeper to sleeper while I used to walk along the side of the line as my legs were not long enough to do that. He would show me around the station and goods yard, I would have rides on the sack barrow and we would go and see the animals in the cattle pens. A walk like this today would be unthinkable and probably dangerous."

It is certainly true that the railways of today are a completely different place compared to 50 or 60 years ago. The days of just wandering onto a platform to watch the comings and goings of station life have sadly gone and it is doubtful that so-called platform tickets (which let you wander around a station without actually boarding a train) even still exist. Now we have a lot more security with CCTV and ticket barriers at even the most rural of spots. The life and activity you can expect to find on today's railway is different too. The jobs have been whittled down so that roles such as porter and signalman have gone and most stations have combined the ticket and platform duties into a smaller number of staff. And as most freight (if it travels by rail at all) comes in containerised form there is simply no need for goods sidings or cattle pens; and the huge black expanse of the coal yard, once a common scene at all railway stations, disappeared long, long ago as open fires were gradually phased out.

Brenda was lucky, growing up as she did in a time when the railways were still exciting places and even an average branch line station could be a fascinating place, full of the sights and sounds and smells of a steam railway. Or as Brenda tells me:

"The platform at Rayne station during the age of steam was a really good place to be. To be able to stand there as the loco-motives entered and departed was a wonderful experience."

Sitting here today, in a corner of the old waiting room with people huddled round the open fire, it is just possible to imagine that a train might be due, and that we will end up in a draughty, clanking carriage as the loco whistles and bellows on a trip to wherever our fancy takes us. If it is market day then we could be off to either Dunmow or Bishops Stortford; or then again maybe we could be on a seaside excursion to sunny Clacton. Or perhaps the train is not stopping at all as it's a freight service carrying sugar beet from Felsted to the processing plant, or it might be an early morning milk train loaded with fresh milk from local farms around Rayne, destined to end up in London by 9am. Then again, if it's wartime then it could be a munitions train, shunting slowly through in the dead of night with a deadly cargo, heading for one of the local airfields.

Sadly, those days are long gone. Rayne Station closed on 7 December 1964 and if it were not for the determination of many local people then all that would be left would be memories. Thankfully we have much more than that.

I say goodbye to Brenda and Malcolm and exit the warmth of the cosy waiting room, turning left onto the platform and head towards Braintree. But before I leave, there is just time to check on something. I jump down off the platform-edge onto the track-bed and just before the site of the old signal box I take a good look at the brick wall of the platform. And there it is. It looks like the wall is simply missing a single brick, but actually it is a foot-hole; used by railway workers over the years as an easy way to get on and off the four-foot high platform. It is this foot-hole that Brenda used as a child all of those years ago as a way of getting to and from the signal box. These foot-holes existed on most old platforms and have remained over time. A small thing perhaps, but sometimes it is the small things that can bring memories flooding back.

Things may have changed over the years but at least at Rayne Station there is a small piece of living history that is being preserved for all to see. And if you ever get the chance to visit the Flitch Way then  give yourself a treat and drop in on Rayne Station and order something from the café. Pull up a seat on the platform and then sit back and listen. Is that a train you can hear approaching?

# 10 Closure

*Two views from the old railway in the Felsted area*

I am now on the final stretch of my two-day walk, leaving the former station and railway carriage behind me. I pass Warner Close (named after the old stationmaster, Jim Warner) on my left, go under another old brick bridge at Gore Road, and then finally leave the village behind as the track-bed breaks out into open countryside once again. It is at this point that we should probably consider the final phase in the life of the Bishop's Stortford to Braintree Railway as it heads towards its inevitable decline and fall. The branch line had seen several changes of ownership since its birth in 1869 up until the outbreak of World War Two and along with the rest of the national railway network it was to experience one more upheaval as it reached the 1950s.

At the end of the Second World War the railways were in a dreadful state having suffered from both a lack of funding to repair and replace rolling stock, plus many lines had been wrecked due to enemy attacks. In fact the damage was far greater than that inflicted in World War One where there had been only limited bomb damage. Although the London and North East Railway had drawn up extensive rebuilding plans post war, events nationally were to overtake them when the Labour Government of 1945 decided to take the entire railway network into state ownership. This nationalisation of all the rail services was effectively the end of the days of the 'Big Four' railway companies (including the LNER) and saw instead the creation of British Railways in 1948. Over time the old railway logos and emblems that graced the carriages, locos and buildings of the old companies would be replaced with new insignia, and the only ones to remain (even to this day) are usually those embossed into original buildings and ironwork.

For many of the country's branch lines the immediate post-war period was a bit of a boom time. The rationing of many everyday items (including petrol) continued for many years after the war had ended and this had the effect of reducing car, bus and lorry traffic considerably, and thereby gave a temporary boost to rail traffic. On the Bishops Stortford to Braintree Railway the freight and goods services remained reasonable and the occasional seaside excursion to places like Clacton and Walton-on-the-Naze continued along with the normal passenger service. The line was also seen as a useful diversionary route in case of engineering work on the main line. However, the new management of what was to become (the less than glamorously titled) British Rail, Eastern Region decided to focus on what they considered to be loss-making services by undertaking traffic surveys of various lines, including the Bishops Stortford branch. In 1950 British Rail stated that it was costing twice as much to run the branch line as it was receiving in fares and that on average each train was carrying fewer than nine passengers. They later went on to say that a comparison between local bus and train services had highlighted that in a single week buses carried 7,500 people between Bishops Stortford and Braintree, while only 630 had taken the train.

*LNER timetable from 1940s*

With local buses now embedded in rural areas, offering more frequent and convenient services, and petrol coming off rationing the writing was well and truly on the wall for many branch lines. The poor location of some railway stations, far away from centre of the towns and villages they were supposed to serve, was now cruelly exploited by the much more flexible bus and coach companies. At a public meeting in Dunmow in May 1951, British Railways proposed the closure of the Bishops Stortford to Braintree Railway and despite opposition from both the local MP and Essex County Council, British Railways were adamant that the loss making service should close. Eventually it was proposed that passenger services would cease in March of 1952. The die had been cast and the days of this branch line were well and truly numbered.

*An early British Railways logo*

In the early 1950s many East Anglian branch lines would also close, including the Heachem to Wells and Mundesley to Cromer railways in Norfolk and the Waveney Valley and Mid-Suffolk Light Railways. In Essex the light railways from Elsenham to Thaxted and Kelvedon to Tollesbury were also to carry their last passengers. With the creation of the new nationalised railway network had come a new focus on the costs associated with the running of many of the lesser-used and remote branch lines. And so, at least ten years before Dr Beeching had even thought about sharpening his famous axe, many rural railways were closed down.

The final days for the Bishops Stortford to Braintree Railway were, thanks to its freight services, to be long and drawn out by the standards of other railways. There was to be no sudden death to the whole of the line, and instead it was to be pruned back, piece by piece. First, the passenger service ended on 1 March 1952 when a train packed with locals and enthusiasts set off from Bishops Stortford at 8.15pm, exploding detonators laid on the track as it went. The steam loco (an F5 for enthusiasts) pulled two passenger coaches the 18 miles to Braintree, stopping at all stations along the line and finally arriving at just after 9pm. By all accounts the last train encountered one of the local bus services as it passed close to the railway near Dunmow, and the loco gave out two long, derisory hoots of defiance; a final stand against the dreaded bus service that had proved to be the final nail in its coffin.

With this final departure so came the end of the passenger service. The stations remained open for the conveyance of freight traffic although the staffing levels were reduced accordingly, and the halts at Bannister Green and Stane Street were closed completely. There were also several special services that brought pupils to the private school at Felsted at the beginning and end of each term. Meanwhile the occasional through train to the seaside still made its way along the branch and every now and then a railway enthusiasts' special would explore the railway, stopping at all the stations for photo opportunities and the chance to take a look at the old buildings.

The launch of the much-heralded Modernisation Plan by British Railways took place in 1955. The key elements were the phasing out of steam traction in favour of diesel and electric locomotives, the electrification of large parts of the network and the creation of new marshalling yards for goods traffic. The pros and cons of this plan have been widely discussed in other books and articles but the general consensus is that it didn't work; mainly because of the confused and disorganised way it was handled. The new diesel locos that were commissioned were from different manufacturers, which meant standardisation was not possible, plus there were problems with reliability of many of the new trains. This often led to the embarrassing situation where steam locos were called upon to rescue stranded diesel engines which had broken down. The belief that the old-fashioned goods wagon could somehow be brought into the modern age was also way off the mark as the future would later be shown to be the new containerised form of freight movement, something which Dr Beeching would go on to champion in 1963. In the end the Modernisation Plan was seen as an unsuccessful last attempt to bring the railways up-to-date and perhaps back into profit. Its failure led to the inevitable calls for something even more far-reaching to be considered to rescue the ailing network and those calls would eventually lead to the publication of the Beeching Report and all that was to follow.

But back in the late 1950s and early 1960s, and with passenger travel ended, the problem at the Bishops Stortford to Braintree Railway was all to do with the faltering freight service. March 1957 saw Madeline Scraggs leave her employment as the crossing keeper at Easton Lodge when it was decided that the few trains that still used the railway would have to stop at the crossing and the crew would then open and close the gates themselves. And in 1966 Takeley Station stopped taking coal deliveries and the signal box was removed. In the same year the viaduct that crossed the Chelmer Valley near Dunmow was in such a dilapidated state that trains were forced to reduce their speed to 10mph before venturing across it. Rather than spend a considerable sum on repairs it was decided to condemn the structure and this led to the closure of the line between Dunmow and Felsted. Later (in 1977) the viaduct was demolished using explosive charges leaving a yawning gap across the valley, and has left this section of the Flitch Way hard to follow to this day.

With freight traffic faltering, the railway was not able to run through traffic between Dunmow and Felsted, and the line only ran from Bishops Stortford to Easton Lodge or one side and Felsted and Braintree on the other. Thus, the slow but inexorable move of freight from rail to road continued for several more years until British Sugar decided to stop the railway-bound service and transfer it to lorries in 1969. Finally, in 1970, with no traffic to speak of, the track from Braintree to Felsted was lifted. Then, in 1972 the Geest banana processing plant that had occupied land next to Easton Lodge Halt stopped all of its railway transportation and moved it onto the road as well. All passenger and freight traffic had now stopped on the railway and all that was now left was for one final trip to be made before the line was finally given its last rites.

On the 27 July 1972 a diesel engine left Bishops Stortford pulling a brake van filled with railway enthusiasts. It stopped at Takeley Station and then moved on to Easton Lodge where they got off, took photos, probably bemoaned the loss of another branch line, and the train then finally returned back to Stortford. After 113 years of service and from a very faltering start, the Bishops Stortford to Braintree Railway had finally closed down. Although various projects have been mooted to bring the service back over the years, they have come to nothing and today it would cost a great deal of money to return the railway to this area. However, the final destination of this old branch line at Braintree never lost its station and is still connected to the railway network and it is here that my journey will shortly come to an end.

Day 2, 5pm

The final few miles of the old railway sees the end of the rural stretch of line with Rayne Station a couple of miles behind me. I have to say goodbye to the embankments and cuttings, to the many bridges, stations, villages and hamlets that I have passed over the last 18 miles and take the final stage of my journey into Braintree itself. The old tree-lined track now slowly starts to give way to the occasional house as the outskirts of the town now comes into view.

*Braintree's remaining branch line runs to Liverpool St via Witham*

Braintree, a settlement that goes back over 4,000 years, lies beside the River Brain and this may indicate that the origin of the town's name benefited from being close to the old Roman road called Stane Street. As with Dunmow and Saffron Walden, Braintree is a market town and was granted its charter in 1190. It has been famous over the years as an area for textile manufacture when first it became a centre for the wool trade in the early part of the 19th century and this was to be followed by silk production as well. The famous Courtauld family had a factory here and the celebrated naturalist John Ray lived nearby in Black Notley. The population of Braintree has boomed over the years and proves very clearly that the continued presence of a railway acts as a magnet for growth. In 1871, a few years after the Bishops Stortford branch line came to Braintree, the population was 4,790 and by 1961 this had increased to 20,600. In 2011 this had more than doubled to well over 42,000, and it continues to keep rising to this day. On the outskirts of town is a vast shopping area called Braintree Freeport and it is the kind of shopping village that you might find in the United States. This retail park has spawned its own railway station and has over time helped to swell the population of the area even further. However, the ever-expanding nature of Braintree has not come without cost.

*The Victorian legacy of cast iron still remains at Braintree*

The town is now somewhat sprawling in nature with its boundaries pushing outwards, threatening to engulf the neighbouring villages of Rayne and High Garrett.

This rapid expansion is in no small part due to the continued existence of the railway and the fact that it not only links with the mainline at Witham but also runs through-trains straight to Liverpool Street on most days. Not bad for a branch line that managed to survive the Beeching cuts when so many others did not, and which has since gone on increase its passenger numbers.

Braintree was linked to the railway network in the very early days of train travel when in 1848 the Maldon, Witham and Braintree Railway built a single-track branch line that approached the town from Witham in the east. Opened by those pioneers of East Anglian train travel, the Eastern Counties Railway, the branch crossed the mainline to Liverpool Street at Witham before heading to the port of Maldon on the Blackwater Estuary. For the next 20 years the line came to a buffer-stop at Braintree until 1869 when and the Bishops Stortford branch was constructed, approaching the town from the west. The Eastern Counties' cunning plan to cut Essex in half from east to west and thereby blocking any competitor from crossing its territory was now complete.

With this new role as a through-station, and the expected increase in traffic that would come with it, the station was rebuilt and moved several hundred yards to its current position. Although Braintree Station was built in the same style as other stations such as Felsted and Rayne and the station itself was much larger in size, the familiar sash windows and red brickwork make it unmistakable as another 1865 station. Although some elements of the station have been altered over the years to accommodate new ways of working, several gems from the Great Eastern Railway (GER) period are still very much present. The waiting room still boasts its original open fireplace while the platform canopy, with its intricate ironwork reminiscent of the roof at Liverpool Street, is a wonderful piece of GER architecture that dates back to 1886. In fact the canopy at Braintree is probably one of the best remaining examples of Victorian cast-ironwork anywhere to be found on a branch line station.

Once the Bishops Stortford to Braintree Railway lost its

freight traffic into Braintree in 1969 the station would eventually return to its original buffer-stop status; and then with the general move of freight away from the railway Braintree would go on to lose its goods yard as well. However, all was not lost and thanks to the electrification of the line from Braintree to Witham in 1977, modern rolling stock now provides a fast and efficient service from Braintree, and over 800,000 passenger journeys are made from the station every year. The station and its branch line are a rare example of a railway that managed to escape the clutches of Beeching and to go on to prove that some rural railways can be successful.

Before I jump onto a train that will take me back to Liverpool Street I have one final detour to make into Braintree town. Up and away from the railway station and past the old Embassy Cinema (now turned into a pub) I turn into a long suburban street and a row of terraced houses. Brenda Allard has given me the name of a man who has a hidden secret in the basement of his house; and it is a secret that I am keen to witness.

Ron Hutley opens the front door to his home and leads me into the living room of what is clearly an immaculate house. There are small china pieces and paperweights dotted all around. Ron is 91 years old and lives with his wife Margaret. He still has a good head of fine, white hair and as we talk about his past it is easy to forget Ron's advanced years as he still possesses bright, twinkling eyes and a wide smile.

I ask him about his life and career. "Well, I spent 25 years in the fire brigade" he says, "And before that I was a heavy goods driver in the army."

I know from our discussion that Ron saw service in Germany towards the end of the war and that he was one of the first British servicemen to enter the now infamous Bergen-Belsen concentration camp. He is not keen to dwell on any of the details of his experiences there and this book is probably not the right place to explore such things, but I do not doubt that his memories of that time would have stayed with him until this day. So, I move on to Ron's long-term enjoyment of everything to do with trains. What were his first memories of the local railways?

*Ron Hutley in his basement museum*

"I used to go down to Braintree goods yard and watch all of the trains coming and going. I even used to ride in the driver's cab from time to time!" He says smiling broadly. Then he continues: "Of course, you can't do that sort of thing today. All the cabs are enclosed for one thing, plus all the health and safety stuff has put paid to that."

Perhaps it is all of these trips to the railway that got Ron started with his hobby of collecting things. It is a well kept secret that Ron's mania for keeping all sorts of memorabilia has led to the creation of a sort of unofficial museum, here in his house.

"Would you like to see it?" He asks. And with that he gets

up slowly out of his wing chair and leads me through the hallway to a small wooden door.

He gives me a warning: "Now, mind your step, the staircase is a bit steep."

He flicks a small light-switch that illuminates a set of rickety wooden stairs that lead down into a dark basement below. Ron goes first and although a little unsteady on his feet he manages to negotiate the staircase with ease and disappears down into the gloom from where he presses a few more switches. More lights flicker into life. And as I take the last few steps of the stairs and try to get used to the lower height of the basement ceiling, the room opens up in front of me. In a space that is roughly 15 ft square is an amazing collection of one man's life. Anything that cannot be displayed because of lack of space is neatly stacked in piles or under tables. Everything else, and it is a lot, is on display. Glass cabinets line the walls, the floor is knee-deep in bric-a-brac and suspended from the ceiling are Airfix models. The bulk of the collection is railway related and ranges from old railway gazettes and magazines to full-sized station nameplates that would have adorned the platforms of many a long-lost station. There is a 3ft long white on blue enamel nameplate proclaiming YELDHAM, in a British Rail typeface. Yeldham station closed in 1964 and my guess is that throughout his life Ron made many friends who worked on the railways and they probably helped him to acquire all sorts of station furniture over the years. There is even an old oil lamp with 'Rayne' embossed onto it, which would have been used by the porter or stationmaster to check on the buildings after dark.

There are not just nameplates either. There are all manner of enamelled signs and maps here including: NO ENTRY, GENTLEMEN, DO NOT TRESSPASS ON THE RAILWAY,

GER, LNER and numerous other pieces of railway ephemera adorn all four walls in this basement. And it is not just the walls. Almost every inch of the ceiling has either a model plane or a bit of signage or an old poster attached to it. There are paintings of steam engines, model steam engines galore and, sitting in a giant glass and mahogany case, one of the largest model steam engines I have ever seen. The loco and its tender must be eight  inches high and over four feet long. Two walls are taken up with large glass display cases that contain dozens of smaller engines of all types plus a wonderful assortment of pristine Dinky toys; everything from cars to buses to lorries. And all are laid out, row after row, sitting alongside other eclectic collections that Ron has clearly taken a shine to over the years. There are horse brasses, cigarette cards, AA and RAC badges. Sitting in one corner of the room is another glass case containing a full-size fireman's uniform, perfectly draped around a tailor's dummy. It must be 50 years old and presumably it harks back to Ron's time in the fire service.

This small, unofficial collection of memorabilia has been handled with love and care, where everything from the thinnest magazine to the largest model locomotive looks in pristine condition. I am sure that even at the age of 91, Ron could probably lay his hands on any single item that you could mention, no matter how deeply buried away it was. This is the kind of collection that would be gratefully received by many of the railway museums around the country with open arms – and with good reason. Ron Hutley's private collection may appear to be one man's obsession with the railways but actually it is the accumulation of over 70 years of one man's journey through life. In collecting and hoarding so many items of the seemingly mundane Ron has actually managed to keep hold of a snapshot of everyday life. He meticulously filed away the day-to-day bits and pieces that many of us do not give a second thought to. The toys we used to play with or the signs we used to pass at the local railway station do not always mean very much to us, until they are gone. Then suddenly we seem to long for them all over again. Luckily the old pieces of railway furniture are extremely hard-wearing and, being made from iron, will usually withstand the ravages of time very well. Enamel signs are also very tough and weatherproof, which means that after a proper cleaning they will be good for another 100 years or more, as long as they are in good hands. And here, in a small suburban terraced house in Braintree they certainly are in very good hands.

Although I would love to stay a while longer I am aware that it is now well after 6pm and with the daylight fading I really do need to rush for the next train out of Braintree. I thank Ron for the guided tour of his little museum and leave him standing on the doorstep of his house. With a wave and a cheery smile he wishes me a safe journey as I head back to the station and the end of my journey.

The remaining branch line from Braintree to Witham survived Beeching and today runs modern electric multiple units (EMUs) along its single track. After leaving Braintree the train stops at Braintree Freeport (serving the shoppers and workers at the retail park) before moving on to stations at both Cressing and White Notley, finally reaching the mainline at Witham, just over six miles away. These trains are fast, efficient, comfortable and, let's be honest, quite boring really. The new air-conditioned rolling stock may glide effortlessly over welded track while you sit on a comfortable (if rather narrow) cushioned seat, but the trains of today lack any sense of character. But travel today is not about character.

The trains of today are all about speed and getting from A to B as quickly as possible. The benefits of getting the Eurostar from St Pancras to Paris and Brussels are built around it being able to compete with airlines; to do that it has to travel very fast, with few stops. Another ultra-fast service is the controversial new railway from London to Birmingham (HS2), which will allow trains to travel at up to 250mph between the two cities and shave up to 30 minutes off the journey time. For these inter-city routes speed really is of the essence. A faster journey time not only allows passengers to get to their destination more quickly but it allows for more trains to use the same piece of track; and providing there is an up-to-date signalling system in place, then more frequent services can be run. More trains, travelling faster, carrying more passengers than ever before. This is the inter-city dream that Dr Beeching was hoping to achieve in the early 1960s. His essential argument that the branch lines were unprofitable, disorganised, and that there were too many of them anyway, and that all efforts should be put into the mainline (or inter-city) network, is to a greater extent exactly where we are today.

The East Coast route from Kings Cross to Edinburgh, the West Coast route from Euston to Glasgow and the mainline from Paddington to the South West are all at various stages of upgrade to allow faster, more frequent services. Meanwhile long overdue electrification, first talked of during the Modernisation Plan of the 1950s, is also underway on various lines and the delivery of more streamlined and faster trains is now a regular occurrence. Of course, the fragmented nature of the railway franchises may lead to a disjointed system, and the network may be patchy with investment still required in many places. But it is still a network that Beeching would probably recognise if he were around today. And although we are way behind the other countries who invested heavily in their inter-city services many years ago (think of the French high speed trains) there is every reason to believe that the UK has a bright future as far as inter-city is concerned.

But for branch line Britain the journey has never really been about speed. The Bishops Stortford to Braintree Railway ran for 18 miles and had eight stations or halts along the way. This means a train would be stopping every couple of miles, and if it wasn't doing that it was either slowing to approach a station or accelerating to leave one. Very little time was spent actually at speed along this branch - or any other branch for that matter. Perhaps it is this curious nature of branch lines that makes them so endearing to so many people. Travelling at a slower speed leaves time for reflection and considera-tion, two things sadly missing in today's fast-moving society. The fact that a train stops at every station and does not just hurtle through at speed need not be a disadvantage. A stop-ping train gives us all new places to explore, even if it is only a small town or village. And if you look out of the window of a train travelling at a leisurely pace you will see much more than you ever would from an express; where everything except objects in the far distance become a speeding blur. As that famous traveller and TV personality Michael Palin once declared: 'If travelling is worth doing, it's worth doing at a leisurely manner.'

Branch lines have a character all of their own and even the disused and forgotten ones, like the Bishops Stortford to Braintree, still leave a lasting impression on both the physical landscape and the people who remember them fondly. Perhaps this is because of the profound changes that the coming of a railway meant to these quiet rural areas. Whether that was by giving people the opportunity to travel for the first time, or by allowing the movement of goods and freight, or by providing a whole new set of employment opportunities, from driver to stationmaster. The coming of the railways created a whole new way of life. It was a life that revolved around trains and timetables, with its own culture and language. And you didn't need to work on the railways to appreciate this. Over time the railways found a special place in the hearts of many people and it was to be a place that very other forms of transport could touch. The early railways, even those like the Bishops Stortford to Braintree that had been built with little chance of ever making a profit, became part of daily life. And even when they finally closed down there was always that peculiarly British way of not wanting to let go of it. This is a kind of 'it may be gone but it must not be forgotten' sort of attitude that gives rise to numerous societies, charities and museums up and down the country.

This affinity with the rural branch line is something unique to the British way of life and is probably rooted in many things. The fact that it was a steam service and therefore attracted the fascination of countless young boys (and probably just as many men) must have had something to do with it. Also, being immortalised in old movies such as *The Titfield Thunderbolt, Oh, Mr Porter, Brief Encounter, Strangers on a Train* and *The Railway Children* must also have helped shape our memories and feelings towards this most romantic form of travel. However, for those people who remember steam travel first hand or those who worked all their lives on the railways then the attraction of branch lines needs no explanation.

The original working title for this book was 'Railway People' and although it is neither as memorable or catchy as the final 'Lost and Found' that you have just finished reading, I still feel in some way it is a more accurate title. Because only on a branch line like this would you meet people like Madeline Scraggs, who has such a fondness for the old crossingkeeper's cottage at Easton Lodge that she still lives there. And only on a branch line would you find people like the Friends of the Flitch Way, who do their best to keep some of its old railway history alive through renovation and station rebuilding. People like Brenda Allard and Ron Hutley have both been touched by this railway to such an extent that much of their lives have been spent either exploring it or trying to retain and cherish parts of it. This is the kind of connection and bond that you don't get with any other form of transport and it is the kind of bond that is very hard to break.

*This photo from 1952 (taken between Hockrill Halt and Stortford) is evocative of so many long-lost branch lines (P Paye)*

# 11 Follow the Author

If reading this book has inspired you to pull on your walking boots and head off in the direction of the Flitch Way then please read on and I will try to give you some inside knowledge into making the most out of your trip. What follows is my guide to walking the entire railway from one end (Bishops Stortford) to the other (Braintree) but you can, of course, simply make up your own trip to specific parts of the railway. Either way my only recommendations would be firstly, that you take a pair of good walking shoes or boots as some areas can get muddy in wet weather, and secondly take the relevant Ordnance Survey map (195). This will not only show you the course of the old railway but it will also point out public footpaths and rights-of-way.

If you intend to use public transport to start and finish your journey you will find regular train services to both Braintree and Bishops Stortford and, as you now know, both towns can be easily reached from Liverpool Street. The route of the old Bishops Stortford to Braintree Railway is around 18 miles in length and while most of it is walkable there are specific places where you need to take care otherwise you may end up lost. The first couple of miles of the old branch line (from Stortford to the M11 motorway) can no longer be followed as the track has long since disappeared; however with a little research on the internet (where various people have posted walking routes) or with a copy of Ordnance Survey map 195, the public footpaths will be clearly marked. You should be aiming to cross the M11 by way of a small farm crossing and then follow the footpath as it descends on farmland towards a small lane. Here you will see the single-arch brick bridge of the former railway at Start Hill. Now climb the embankment, walk across the bridge and follow the Flitch Way straight ahead as your walk along the old Bishops Stortford to Braintree Railway really begins.

This walk can be completed in either a single day at a relatively fast walking pace or you can tackle it at a more leisurely pace over a two day period and enjoy stopping off to visit various towns and villages in north Essex. For the two-day walk Great Dunmow will make the ideal overnight stop as it not only marks the half way point of the Flitch Way but it also has several hotels plus good restaurants and pubs.

Start Hill to Dunmow (8 miles)
This is a relatively straightforward walk as you pass Hatfield Forest (footpaths lead into the forest from here) and then pass the villages of Takeley and Little Canfield. Good pubs include the Green Man at Takeley and the Lion and Lamb at Little Canfield – both are short walks from the old railway. You will approach Dunmow via the area called Dunmow Cutting, which is a haven for wildlife and then the footpath comes to an abrupt halt as the busy road (Dunmow Bypass) cuts across the old railway. From here it is a short walk into the town. Much of the centre of Dunmow is a conservation area and it is here that you will find various places to eat, drink or sleep. If you wish to visit the Maltings Museum please remember that it has limited opening times, so please check ahead of your visit. Around a mile outside Dunmow is the small hamlet of Little Easton where the Gardens of Easton Lodge and the beautiful Little Easton Church are situated. The gardens will only have limited opening hours but the church may well be open and is well worth a visit.

Dunmow to Braintree (9 miles)
Your first task will be to pick up the route of the Flitch Way

and this is best done using the OS map. From personal experience (as you will have read in this book) finding the footpath may not be clear, however, if you walk south out of town and head for the Chelmsford Road then you should be able to pick up either Flitch Way signposts or a footpath sign that will bring you back onto the old railway. The route towards Braintree offers some of the best views of the entire walk across rolling farmland and will take you past Felsted. If you have time then it is well worth a detour into the village, which has several pubs and small shops. Once back on the Flitch Way there is a slight detour at Felsted Station as the railway bridge was dismantled long ago, leaving you to cross the main road to rejoin the footpath. Now it is a lovely walk to the restored Rayne Station and its museum and café and then a further two miles of the Flitch Way, which will bring you to Braintree and then end of the line.

David Gridley